Test-Taker's Checklist
for the TSWE

Basic Strategies

Budget your time. Work swiftly; don't linger over difficult questions.

Guess intelligently. Random guessing will probably not raise your score. Do guess if you can eliminate one or more answers.

Save the hardest or most time-consuming questions for last.

Do questions 1-25 and 41-50 before doing questions 26-40.

Mark answers clearly, accurately. Be especially watchful of the number of the question you are answering.

Check the numbering of your answer sheet. Erase cleanly; leave no stray marks.

Look for These Errors:

The Run-on Sentence

The Sentence Fragment

Error in the Case of a Noun or Pronoun

Error in Agreement between Subject and Verb

Error in Agreement between Pronoun and Antecedent

Error in the Tense of the Verb

Failure to use the Subjunctive Mood when required

Error in the Comparison of Adjectives

Confusion in the use of Adjectives and Adverbs

Use of Dangling Modifiers

Lack of Parallel Structure

Error in Diction or Idiom

Remember

Approximately eight to twelve questions do not have an error. Do not waste time looking for obscure errors.

BARRON'S

How to Prepare for the Test of Standard Written English

Sharon Green
Instructor, Merritt College
Oakland, California

Mitchel Weiner
Formerly Member, Department of English
James Madison High School, Brooklyn, New York

Barron's Educational Series, Inc.

All inquiries should be addressed to:
Barron's Educational Series, Inc.
250 Wireless Boulevard
Hauppauge, New York 11788

Library of Congress Catalog Card No. 82-6721
International Standard Book No. 0-8120-2095-2

Library of Congress Cataloging in Publication Data
Green, Sharon.
   Barron's test of standard written English (SAT)
   1. English language—Examinations. 2. Scholastic
aptitude test—Study guides. I. Weiner, Mitchel,
1907–. II. Barron's Educational Series, Inc.
III. Title.
PE1114.G77   428'.0076   82-6721
ISBN 0-8120-2095-2   AACR2
PRINTED IN THE UNITED STATES OF AMERICA

345   410   9876

contents

preface

This book joins its predecessors, *Barron's Mathematical Workbook for College Entrance Examinations* and *Barron's Verbal Aptitude Workbook for College Entrance Examinations* as a source of additional study material to supplement the preparation provided for the SAT in *Barron's How to Prepare for College Entrance Examinations (SAT)*.

Students and teachers will find that this book provides a thorough preparation for the Test of Standard Written English portion of the SAT. Not only does it have a Diagnostic Test and five Typical Tests which have been tried with success in the classroom, but it also includes a three-chapter section devoted to the principles of grammar and usage tested in this part of the SAT. Students taking the six tests in this book will find the explanation of answers and the Charts which refer them to the pages where each topic is discussed in the Grammar and Usage chapters very helpful.

We are grateful to the many individuals who have assisted us in the preparation of this book. Mr. Alan Fambrini and Mr. Daryl Christianer provided invaluable technical assistance and Ms. Josia Jackson's secretarial help was indispensable. We are indebted to Ms. Ruth Pecan, Ms. Carole Berglie, and Mr. Karl Weber of Barron's Educational Series, Inc. for their excellent editorial guidance.

S.W.G.

M.W.

getting acquainted with the Test of Standard Written English

part one

chapter 1

questions often asked about the Test of Standard Written English

What Is Standard Written English?

The College Entrance Examination Board, which administers the SAT and the Test of Standard Written English, has indicated that it regards standard written English as "the language of most college textbooks" and as the kind of writing college instructors expect to find in their students' papers. It is, in essence, the kind of writing which is uniform throughout the English-speaking world; it is the language of the "educated" and it is free of slang and colloquialisms. It is writing that is free of errors in agreement, case, tense, mood, voice, diction, and punctuation.

How Is Ability in Standard Written English Tested on the SAT?

The Scholastic Aptitude Test, which is taken by more than a million high school juniors and seniors each year, includes a separately-scored thirty–minute test devoted to testing writing ability. The fifty questions in this section test your ability to recognize errors in usage and to determine which of several choices best expresses an idea. This is the Test of Standard Written English (TSWE).

What Form Do the Test Questions Take?

On most forms of the Test of Standard Written English, questions 1–25 and 41–50 test your ability to recognize errors in usage. Questions 26–40 test your ability to select the best of several ways of expressing an idea. The following brief test, containing 10 items, illustrates the nature of the two kinds of questions. The questions and answers are analyzed. Take this brief test and check the explanations.

sample questions: usage

Directions: In each of the sentences below, there are four underlined words or phrases. If you think there is an error in usage, grammar, diction, or punctuation in one of the underlined parts, write the letter indicated on your answer paper. If there is no error in any of the underlined parts, mark (E) on your answer paper.

1. The aircraft <u>carrier</u> with all her
        A
   <u>accompanying ships</u> <u>are going to</u>
      B   C
   sail to the <u>Persian Gulf</u>. <u>No error</u>
        D   E

2. <u>Let us</u> <u>try</u> to settle this dispute
    A B
   <u>between</u> you and <u>I</u> before we
     C   D
   lose our tempers. <u>No error</u>
         E

3. If he <u>had listened</u> to me when I
      A
   advised <u>him</u>, he <u>would not be in</u>
       B   C
   <u>this</u> mess today. <u>No error</u>
    D   E

4. Neither John <u>or</u> his classmates
         A
   <u>are</u> <u>eager</u> to organize a campaign
    B C
   <u>to raise</u> money for the school
     D
   band. <u>No error</u>
       E

5. After John <u>listened</u> to <u>the speaker</u>
       A   B
   <u>who</u> was expounding on the
    C
   advantages that Nameless College
   <u>offered</u>. <u>No error</u>
    D E

6. <u>Riding</u> through the tunnel, smoke
    A
   filled the <u>subway</u> car and <u>created</u>
      B   C
   a <u>panic</u>. <u>No error</u>
     D E

sample questions: sentence correction

Directions: In each sentence below, some or all of the words are underlined. The portion underlined may be correct or it may contain an error in grammar, diction, style, or punctuation. The sentence is followed by five possible ways of writing the underlined portion. If you think the underlined portion is correct in the original sentence, you will choose (A) as your answer, because (A) repeats the underlined section. If you think the underlined portion is incorrect, you will select the group of words from choices (B), (C), (D), or (E) which best corrects the error you have found. Do not select a choice which changes the meaning of the original sentence.

7. Running far behind the leaders, <u>the favorite found racing room and began</u> to close the gap as the horses neared the far turn.

 (A) the favorite found racing room and began

 (B) racing room was found and the favorite began

 (C) the favorite began by finding racing room

 (D) the favorite had found racing room and began

 (E) the favorite found racing room and had begun

8. If I <u>would have known about the injury to the player, I would not have bet</u> on the game.

    (A) would have known about the injury to the player, I would not have bet
    (B) would of known about the injury to the player, I would not of bet
    (C) had known about the injury to the player, I would not have bet
    (D) would have known about the injury to the player, I should not of bet
    (E) would have known about the injury to the player, I should not have bet

9. <u>He turned on the lights it was still too dark to read.</u>

    (A) He turned on the lights it was still too dark to read.
    (B) He turned on the lights, it was still too dark to read.
    (C) Turning on the lights, it was still too dark to read.
    (D) He turned on the lights; and it was still too dark to read.
    (E) Although he had turned on the lights, it was still too dark to read.

10. Officer Jones <u>is one of the police officers who is going</u> to be cited for bravery at this meeting.

    (A) is one of the police officers who is going
    (B) is one of the police officers who are going
    (C) is a police officer who is going
    (D) is one of the police officers who was going
    (E) is one of the police officers who were going

ANALYSIS OF SAMPLE QUESTIONS

In Part II of this book, you will find a summary of the rules which you should use in determining the reason for your choice of the correct answers. You should become familiar with these rules. As you take the six full–length tests in this book, you will find that the repetition of the kinds of errors that appear on the TSWE will enable you to recognize them when they appear on the actual exam.

Some gifted students are able to identify the error or errors in these questions as soon as they read the sentence. Most of us, however, should not rely on our first impression; we should analyze each of the choices before we select the answer. An analysis of each of the ten questions you have just answered follows.

1. Choice (A) is a noun. It is the subject of the verb *are going*. Since the subject and the verb must agree in person and number, either *carrier* or *are going* is incorrect. Since both are underlined, we must look for additional information before deciding on the choice. The use of *her* in the phrase which follows *carrier* indicates that the subject must be singular and that the verb is incorrect. Choice (C) is the correct answer.

2. Choice (A), *let* is often confused with *leave*. In this sentence, *let* is correct. In choice (B), *try to settle* is better than *try and settle*. The preposition *between* should be used when only two items are mentioned, so choice (C) is correct. Choice (D), *I* is incorrect because the preposition *between* should be followed by a pronoun in the objective case; in this instance, *me*. Choice is the answer.

3. Choices (A), (B), (C), and (D) are correct. Choice (E) is the answer.

4. The correlatives are *either...or* and *neither...nor*. Since *neither* is not underlined, we must change *or* to *nor*. Choice (A) is the answer.

5. Choice (A), *after* is a subordinating conjunction. The clause it introduces should modify an independent clause. Without the independent clause, this group of words is an incomplete sentence—a fragment. The deletion of *after* leaves us with *John listened to the speaker who was expounding on the advantages that Nameless College offered*, which is a good sentence. Choice (A) is the answer.

6. Choice (A), *riding* is a participle. Since it does not have a word to modify in the sentence, it is dangling. Choice (A) is the answer.

7. Choice (B) suffers from an unnecessary shift from the passive voice (*was found*) to the active voice (*began*). Choice (C) changes the meaning of the sentence. The use of the past perfect tense in choices (D) and (E) is incorrect. Choice (A) is the correct answer.

8. Choice (A) is incorrect. The *if* clause calls for the subjunctive mood. Choice (B) is incorrect for the same reason; in addition, *of* is incorrectly used as a substitute for *had*. Choices (D) and (E) are incorrect for the same reasons. Choice (C) is the correct answer.

9. Choice (A) contains two independent clauses: (1) *He turned on the lights*, and (2) *it was still too dark to read*. Since these two clauses are not properly connected, this group of words is a run-on sentence. The comma in choice (B) does not correct the run-on sentence. Either a semicolon or a conjunction can be used to correct the error. However, the use of the semicolon and the conjunction *and* in choice (D) is incorrect. In choice (C) we find a dangling participle. Choice (E) is the correct answer.

10. In choice (A), we have an error in agreement. The antecedent of *who* is *officers* (plural). To agree with the plural pronoun *who*, the verb should be *are going*. Choice (D) is incorrect for the same reason. Choice (E) changes the meaning of the sentence. Choice (B) is the correct answer.

How Are the Test Questions Scored?

Like the other parts of the SAT, the TSWE uses a formula to correct for guesses. After the questions are graded, a *raw score* is found by using the formula:

Raw Score = Number Right − ¼ Number Wrong

The raw score is converted to a *scaled score* which is reported to the student. For the verbal and mathematical parts of the SAT, the scaled scores range from a minimum of 200 to a maximum of 800. For the TSWE, the scaled score ranges from a minimum of 20 to a maximum of 60+. The purpose of the TSWE is to discover whether a student has the ability to write the kind of English needed for success in college work. It is, therefore, unnecessary to discover the degree of excellence a student has in written English. This is why the highest score is 60+; the TSWE is not sufficiently difficult to separate the student who could score 60 from the student who could score 70 or 80. All of these well-prepared students will be lumped together under the score of 60+. Colleges which want a more precise measure of a student's ability in written English will ask him or her to take the 60–minute English Composition Achievement Test. This Achievement Test is marked on a scale of 200 to 800.

How about Guessing?

The College Board statement that haphazard guessing may result in a lower score should not be disregarded. However, you must not overlook their statement, "When you know that one or more choices can be eliminated, guessing from among the remaining choices should be to your advantage."

Most students who have taken the TSWE report that they can narrow the number of choices to two on many of the questions. At such times, your chances of improving your score far exceed the danger of lowering it. On the TSWE, you will have more opportunities to eliminate choices than on the verbal and mathematical parts. If you can eliminate any of the choices, guess.

What Do Colleges Do with the SAT and TSWE Scores?

According to the College Entrance Examination Board, the scores on the verbal and mathematical parts are to be used by colleges in determining whether an applicant will be accepted. The TSWE score is not considered part of the admissions test. Its primary use is to provide the college with information needed to assign the student to the most appropriate freshman English course. However, this is no reason for complacency. You should try to get as high a score as possible on the TSWE, as well as on the Verbal and Mathematics tests. A poor score on any part of the test cannot help your chances of admission to the college of your choice.

How Can This Book Help You Improve Your TSWE Score?

The Diagnostic Test in Chapter 2, the review of the fundamentals of English grammar and usage in Chapters 3–5, and the five typical tests in Chapters 6 through 10 provide sufficient practice to help you improve. If you read the explanations which accompany each test and review the items which gave you trouble by studying Chapters 3–5, you should find your score improving after a very few hours with this book.

answer sheet-diagnostic test

To the student:

Take the following test under examination conditions.

Have on hand a supply of #2 pencils and a good eraser.

Limit yourself to thirty minutes.

Because you will be penalized for wrong answers, do not guess wildly. However, if you can eliminate some of the choices, you can improve your score by guessing.

The answer grid below is provided for your convenience. Fill in the oval which contains the letter of your choice. You may remove this page from the book for ease in marking your answers.

1. Ⓐ Ⓑ Ⓒ Ⓓ Ⓔ   14. Ⓐ Ⓑ Ⓒ Ⓓ Ⓔ   27. Ⓐ Ⓑ Ⓒ Ⓓ Ⓔ   40. Ⓐ Ⓑ Ⓒ Ⓓ Ⓔ
2. Ⓐ Ⓑ Ⓒ Ⓓ Ⓔ   15. Ⓐ Ⓑ Ⓒ Ⓓ Ⓔ   28. Ⓐ Ⓑ Ⓒ Ⓓ Ⓔ   41. Ⓐ Ⓑ Ⓒ Ⓓ Ⓔ
3. Ⓐ Ⓑ Ⓒ Ⓓ Ⓔ   16. Ⓐ Ⓑ Ⓒ Ⓓ Ⓔ   29. Ⓐ Ⓑ Ⓒ Ⓓ Ⓔ   42. Ⓐ Ⓑ Ⓒ Ⓓ Ⓔ
4. Ⓐ Ⓑ Ⓒ Ⓓ Ⓔ   17. Ⓐ Ⓑ Ⓒ Ⓓ Ⓔ   30. Ⓐ Ⓑ Ⓒ Ⓓ Ⓔ   43. Ⓐ Ⓑ Ⓒ Ⓓ Ⓔ
5. Ⓐ Ⓑ Ⓒ Ⓓ Ⓔ   18. Ⓐ Ⓑ Ⓒ Ⓓ Ⓔ   31. Ⓐ Ⓑ Ⓒ Ⓓ Ⓔ   44. Ⓐ Ⓑ Ⓒ Ⓓ Ⓔ
6. Ⓐ Ⓑ Ⓒ Ⓓ Ⓔ   19. Ⓐ Ⓑ Ⓒ Ⓓ Ⓔ   32. Ⓐ Ⓑ Ⓒ Ⓓ Ⓔ   45. Ⓐ Ⓑ Ⓒ Ⓓ Ⓔ
7. Ⓐ Ⓑ Ⓒ Ⓓ Ⓔ   20. Ⓐ Ⓑ Ⓒ Ⓓ Ⓔ   33. Ⓐ Ⓑ Ⓒ Ⓓ Ⓔ   46. Ⓐ Ⓑ Ⓒ Ⓓ Ⓔ
8. Ⓐ Ⓑ Ⓒ Ⓓ Ⓔ   21. Ⓐ Ⓑ Ⓒ Ⓓ Ⓔ   34. Ⓐ Ⓑ Ⓒ Ⓓ Ⓔ   47. Ⓐ Ⓑ Ⓒ Ⓓ Ⓔ
9. Ⓐ Ⓑ Ⓒ Ⓓ Ⓔ   22. Ⓐ Ⓑ Ⓒ Ⓓ Ⓔ   35. Ⓐ Ⓑ Ⓒ Ⓓ Ⓔ   48. Ⓐ Ⓑ Ⓒ Ⓓ Ⓔ
10. Ⓐ Ⓑ Ⓒ Ⓓ Ⓔ   23. Ⓐ Ⓑ Ⓒ Ⓓ Ⓔ   36. Ⓐ Ⓑ Ⓒ Ⓓ Ⓔ   49. Ⓐ Ⓑ Ⓒ Ⓓ Ⓔ
11. Ⓐ Ⓑ Ⓒ Ⓓ Ⓔ   24. Ⓐ Ⓑ Ⓒ Ⓓ Ⓔ   37. Ⓐ Ⓑ Ⓒ Ⓓ Ⓔ   50. Ⓐ Ⓑ Ⓒ Ⓓ Ⓔ
12. Ⓐ Ⓑ Ⓒ Ⓓ Ⓔ   25. Ⓐ Ⓑ Ⓒ Ⓓ Ⓔ   38. Ⓐ Ⓑ Ⓒ Ⓓ Ⓔ
13. Ⓐ Ⓑ Ⓒ Ⓓ Ⓔ   26. Ⓐ Ⓑ Ⓒ Ⓓ Ⓔ   39. Ⓐ Ⓑ Ⓒ Ⓓ Ⓔ

chapter 2

---

diagnostic test

Time: 30 minutes

Directions: In each of the sentences below, there are four underlined words or phrases. If you think there is an error in usage, grammar, diction, or punctuation in one of the underlined parts, write the letter indicated on your answer paper. If there is no error in any of the underlined parts, mark (E) on your answer paper.

Example: The aircraft carrier with all her accompanying ships are going to sail to the
A   B   C

Persian Gulf. No error
D   E
The correct answer is (C).

---

1. When the litigants first met in the
    A
    lawyer's office, the plaintiff
    B
    refuses to respond to her
    C   D
    opponent's greeting. No error
    E

2. Estragon, eldest of the heirs of
    A
    Basil, were renowned not only for
    B   C
    his scholarship but also for his

    piety. No error
    D   E

3. This package contains Form 1040,
    A
    related forms and schedules, and
    B
    the instructions needed to
    C   D
    complete them. No error
    E

4. The President learned of the
    A
    newest snag in the negotiations
    B
    to free the hostages, which made
    C
    him very unhappy. No error
    D   E

5. Prancing Prince, Blackie, and Mr.

   J. <u>finished</u> in a tie for first place
   A

   in the stake race, <u>but</u> the <u>former</u>
   B   C

   was disqualified for <u>bearing out</u>
   D

   in the stretch. <u>No error</u>
   E

6. You can see <u>how</u> he
   A

   plays his position aggressively

   and <u>without fear</u> <u>if</u> you
   B   C

   watch the action in the

   line <u>instead of</u> following the
   D

   ball. <u>No error</u>
   E

7. The wait seemed <u>endlessly</u>; our
   A

   patience <u>was exhausted</u> before
   B

   we <u>were permitted</u> to <u>board</u> the
   C   D

   plane. <u>No error</u>
   E

8. You are a <u>malingerer</u>; I know you
   A

   are <u>constantly</u> <u>laying</u> down on
   B   C

   the job and <u>postponing</u> doing
   D

   your chores. <u>No error</u>
   E

9. The best way <u>to explain</u> how this
   A

   procedure is expected <u>to work</u> is
   B

   to explain how it actually <u>worked</u>
   C

   when it was <u>first tried</u>. <u>No error</u>
   D   E

10. <u>Talking</u> incessantly <u>throughout</u>
    A   B

    the magnificent dinner <u>which</u> Mr.
    C

    Alexander <u>had prepared</u> for his
    D

    distinguished guests from France.

    <u>No error</u>
    E

11. If we are <u>to appear</u> in
    A   B

    alphabetical order, Mary Lincoln

    <u>should perform</u> after John Jones,
    C

    Stanley Kaye and <u>I</u>. <u>No error</u>
    D   E

12. <u>If President Carter</u>
    A

    <u>would have signed</u> the bill, we
    B

    <u>would not be facing</u> <u>such</u>
    C   D

    serious problems of inflation

    today. <u>No error</u>
    E

13. When he heard the news <u>about</u>
    A

    the <u>surrender</u> of the enemy, he
    B

    <u>opens</u> a bottle of champagne to
    C

    toast the <u>coming</u> of peace.
    D

    <u>No error</u>
    E

14. The Chrysler Corporation

    announced that <u>it</u> was facing
    A

    bankruptcy and <u>insists</u> that <u>only</u>
    B   C

    governmental aid <u>could save</u> it.
    D

    <u>No error</u>
    E

15. <u>Among</u> the marathon runners
    A

    who <u>finished</u> in the first group of
    B

    fifty <u>were</u> John, Henry, and <u>me</u>.
    C   D

    <u>No error</u>
    E

16. The marauding bandits <u>which</u>
    A

    were attacking the isolated farms

    and ranches <u>were</u> <u>finally</u>
    B   C

    captured when the sheriff

    <u>organized</u> a posse. <u>No error</u>
    D   E

17. The <u>lengthy</u> conversation
    A
    between the officer <u>who had</u>
    B
    arrested the intruder and <u>he</u>
    C
    finally ended, and they turned
    their attention to <u>me</u>. <u>No error</u>
    D   E

18. The island was <u>so</u> <u>bleak</u> that it
    A B
    <u>could sustain</u> very little life of <u>any</u>
    C   D
    kind. <u>No error</u>
    E

19. He <u>was</u> an <u>excellent</u> student, an
    A   B
    <u>outstanding</u> athlete, and <u>was</u> the
    C   D
    most popular member of his
    fraternity. <u>No error</u>
    E

20. He was enamored <u>by</u> her wit, her
    A
    charm, and, <u>especially</u>, her
    B
    sympathy for the sick and
    <u>maimed</u> people <u>whom</u> she
    C   D
    helped. <u>No error</u>
    E

21. <u>Provided</u> he <u>raises</u> the money
    A   B
    <u>needed</u> for the project by noon
    C
    tomorrow, <u>I will gladly join</u> him
    D
    in this activity. <u>No error</u>
    E

22. The <u>Siamese</u> cat <u>who</u> won first
    A   B
    prize at the Webster Show
    <u>had not won</u> a ribbon in five
    C
    <u>earlier</u> competitions. <u>No error</u>
    D   E

23. Mr. Smith, the <u>principal</u> of our
    A
    school, is one of the candidates
    <u>who</u> <u>is</u> being considered for <u>city</u>
    B C   D
    superintendent. <u>No error</u>
    E

24. To meet the needs <u>for</u> all <u>our</u>
    A   B
    students, we need <u>to improve</u> our
    C
    shops and laboratories <u>as well as</u>
    D
    the library. <u>No error</u>
    E

25. When the fire gong <u>sounded</u>, the
    A
    teacher <u>insisted upon</u> the
    B
    <u>pupils' lining up</u> in an orderly
    C
    fashion <u>before</u> leaving the
    D
    building. <u>No error</u>
    E

Directions: In each sentence below, some or all of the words are underlined. The portion underlined may be correct or it may contain an error in grammar, diction, style, or punctuation. The sentence is followed by five possible ways of writing the underlined portion. If you think the underlined portion is correct in the original sentence, you will choose (A) as your answer, because (A) repeats the underlined section. If you think the underlined portion is incorrect, you will select the group of words from choices (B), (C), (D) or (E) which best corrects the error you have found. Do not select a choice which changes the meaning of the original sentence.

Example: Although I calculate that he will be here any minute, I cannot wait much longer for him to arrive.

  (A) Although I calculate that he will be here

  (B) Although I reckon that he will be here

  (C) Because I calculate that he will be here

  (D) Although I am confident that he will be here

  (E) Because I am confident that he will be here

  The correct answer is (D).

---

26. Since John is taller than any other boy in his class, he should try out for the basketball team.

  (A) Since John is taller than any other boy

  (B) Since John is the tallest of any boy

  (C) Since John is taller than any boy

  (D) Inasmuch as John is taller than any boy

  (E) Because of John's being taller than any boy

27. Nearing the two-minute mark, the game was tied; it was likely to go into overtime.

  (A) Nearing the two-minute mark

  (B) When nearing the two-minute mark

  (C) As we approached the two-minute mark

  (D) Upon nearing the two-minute mark

  (E) Reaching the two-minute mark

28. It is possible for a student to do well in class all semester and then you fail because of a poor performance on the final examination.

  (A) then you fail

  (B) then one fails

  (C) then you get a failing grade

  (D) later he fails

  (E) then to fail

29. One phase of the business cycle is the expansion phase, this phase is a two-fold one, including recovery and prosperity.

  (A) expansion phase, this

  (B) expansion phase, which

  (C) expansion phase, because this

(D)   expansion phase; this

(E)   expansion phase. this

30.   For seven-year-old Maria da Silva, of Recife, Brazil, the most exciting thing about her first day at the Vasco da Gama School was not the new school building itself, with its well-lighted classrooms and modern equipment, but the lunch she received there.

(A)   For seven-year-old Maria da Silva, of Recife, Brazil, the most exciting thing about her first day at the Vasco da Gama School was not the new school building itself, with its well-lighted classrooms and modern equipment, but the lunch she received there.

(B)   When seven-year-old Maria da Silva, of Recife, Brazil, entered the new building of the Vasco da Gama School, the lunch she received there was more exciting to her than her new surroundings.

(C)   Entering the new building at the Vasco da Gama School at Recife, Brazil, seven-year-old Maria da Silva's most exciting experience was the lunch she received.

(D)   The lunch seven-year-old Maria da Silva of Recife, Brazil, received was more exciting than any aspect of the new building of the Vasco da Gama School.

(E)   To seven-year-old Maria da Silva, the new Vasco da Gama School with its well-lighted classrooms and modern equipment was exciting, but the lunch she received was more exciting.

31.   Most people will agree that the discovery and introduction of modern medicine during the past thirty years has been one of the most important elements in making life longer and that we live more comfortably.

(A)   that we live more comfortably

(B)   that we will live more comfortably

(C)   more comfortable

(D)   more comfortably

(E)   most comfortably

32.   After managing the team for several years, its operation was understood by him.

(A)   its operation was understood by him

(B)   he understood its operation

(C)   an understanding of the operation came to him

(D)   he understood how they operated

(E)   he understood how the team should be operated

33.   Bullied by his wife and intimidated by policemen and parking lot attendants alike, daydreaming about being a surgeon, a crack pistol shot, and so on, enable Walter Mitty to cope with the real world.

(A)   daydreaming about being a surgeon, a crack pistol shot, and so on, enable Walter Mitty to cope with the real world

(B)   daydreaming about being a surgeon, a crack pistol shot, and so on, enables Walter Mitty to cope with the real world

(C)   Walter Mitty reacts to the real world by his daydreams of being a surgeon, a crack pistol shot, and so on

(D)   Walter Mitty escapes from the real world by his daydreams of being a surgeon, a crack pistol shot, and so on

(E)   Walter Mitty is able to cope with the real world by daydreaming of being a surgeon, a crack pistol shot, and so on

34. While walking along the road, a car traveling more than sixty miles an hour nearly struck me.

   (A)   While walking along the road, a car traveling more than sixty miles an hour nearly struck me.

   (B)   While walking along the road, a car traveling faster than sixty miles an hour nearly hit me.

   (C)   While walking along the road, I was nearly hit by a car and it was traveling faster than sixty miles an hour.

   (D)   I was nearly hit by a car traveling faster than sixty miles an hour while I was walking along the road.

   (E)   I was nearly hit by a car traveling more than sixty miles per hour while walking along the road.

35. Government authorities maintain that tremendous savings in the consumption of gasoline would be achieved if speeding was to be limited to 55 miles per hour.

   (A)   speeding was to be limited to 55 miles per hour

   (B)   motorists limited their speed to 55 miles per hour

   (C)   speeding did not exceed 55 miles per hour

   (D)   a motorist was to limit his speed to 55 miles per hour

   (E)   speeding by motorists was to be limited to 55 miles per hour

36. A placebo is sometimes used by a doctor to reassure a difficult patient and making him feel that he is getting proper medical attention.

   (A)   and making him feel

   (B)   and causing him to feel

   (C)   and to make him to feel

   (D)   by making him feel

   (E)   by making him to realize

37. The first of a number of receptions and testimonial dinners for departing Oakland schools' superintendent Ruth B. Love have been scheduled, with more events still in the planning stage.

   (A)   have been scheduled, with more events still

   (B)   have been scheduled, and with more events still

   (C)   has been scheduled, and with more events still

   (D)   has been scheduled, with more events still

   (E)   have been scheduled with more events still

38. Most people earned a poor living as farmers, and they were at the mercy of disease, the elements, and backbreaking labor.

   (A)   disease, the elements, and backbreaking labor

   (B)   disease, and the elements, and they survived only through backbreaking labor

   (C)   disease, the elements, and of backbreaking labor

   (D)   disease, and they survived the elements and backbreaking labor

   (E)   disease, the elements, and the backbreaking labor which was devastating

39. His work as chairman is limited to the calling of meetings of the executive board and <u>to appoint committee members</u>.

    (A) to appoint committee members

    (B) to assign members to committees

    (C) the appointment of committee members

    (D) to name committee members

    (E) the appointment to committees of members

40. The reason for my tardiness was <u>due to the fact that the bus was delayed by heavy traffic</u>.

    (A) due to the fact that the bus was delayed by heavy traffic

    (B) because the bus was delayed by heavy traffic

    (C) that the bus was delayed by heavy traffic

    (D) due to the fact that heavy traffic delayed the bus

    (E) that the delay of my bus was caused by heavy traffic

Directions: In each of the sentences below, there are four underlined words or phrases. If you think there is an error in usage, grammar, diction, or punctuation in any of the underlined parts, write the letter indicated on your answer paper. If there is no error in any of the underlined parts, mark (E) on your answer paper.

> **Example:** The aircraft <u>carrier</u> with all her <u>accompanying</u> ships are <u>going</u> to sail to the
>   A   B   C
> <u>Persian Gulf</u>. <u>No error</u>
>   D   E
> The correct answer is (C).

41. At the end of the reign of King Basil, his kingdom <u>was divided</u> (A) <u>between</u> his three nephews, sons (B) of his sister the Duchess of Arval, <u>who</u> predeceased her brother by (C) <u>less than a month</u>. <u>No error</u> (D) (E)

42. Most reporters were <u>unaware</u> of (A) (B) President <u>Nixon</u> going to visit the (C) Arab leaders <u>until</u> they noticed (D) his absence from the plane which was taking them back to the United States. <u>No error</u> (E)

43. In return <u>of</u> your patience and (A) understanding <u>in this matter</u>, our (B) company has decided <u>to extend</u> (C) your subscription for an <u>additional</u> (D) six months. <u>No error</u> (E)

44. This campaign, <u>first</u> called a (A) (B) police action, resulted in a war <u>notorious</u> for <u>their</u> large numbers (C) (D) of casualties and men missing in action. <u>No error</u> (E)

45. At Atlantic Auto Sales, <u>concerned</u>
    A
    motorists <u>don't have to insist on</u>
    B
    the <u>very best</u> service for their car
    C
    <u>because</u> the very best service is
    D
    the only kind available. <u>No error</u>
    E

46. The bus <u>will not leave</u> for the
    A
    stadium <u>until</u> the players and the
    B
    coach are <u>altogether</u> in the
    C
    terminal and are <u>ready</u> to depart.
    D
    <u>No error</u>
    E

47. The engineer <u>chiefly</u> responsible
    A
    <u>for</u> the <u>development of</u>
    B   C
    our company's floppy disks
    <u>had began</u> his experiments while
    D
    a student at Stanford University.
    <u>No error</u>
    E

48. Scholars have <u>definitely</u>
    A
    established a connection <u>between</u>
    B
    <u>certain texts</u> and the <u>manuscript</u>
    C   D
    at Gertsey. <u>No error</u>
    E

49. <u>When he came</u> to the <u>turnpike</u>
    A   B
    toll gate, he <u>throws</u> his quarter
    C
    <u>into</u> the wire basket in the "Exact
    D
    Change" lane. <u>No error</u>
    E

50. The spraying of malathion <u>in the</u>
    A
    infested areas <u>is expected</u> to
    B
    eliminate the Mediterranean fruit
    fly, but the <u>affect</u> it will have on
    C
    human beings is <u>uncertain.</u>
    D
    <u>No error</u>
    E

STOP
END OF DIAGNOSTIC TEST

Answer Key—Diagnostic Test

1.	**C**	11.	**D**	21.	**E**	31.	**C**	41.	**B**
2.	**B**	12.	**B**	22.	**B**	32.	**B**	42.	**C**
3.	**E**	13.	**C**	23.	**C**	33.	**E**	43.	**A**
4.	**C**	14.	**B**	24.	**B**	34.	**D**	44.	**D**
5.	**C**	15.	**D**	25.	**E**	35.	**B**	45.	**E**
6.	**B**	16.	**A**	26.	**A**	36.	**D**	46.	**C**
7.	**A**	17.	**C**	27.	**C**	37.	**D**	47.	**D**
8.	**C**	18.	**E**	28.	**E**	38.	**A**	48.	**E**
9.	**E**	19.	**D**	29.	**D**	39.	**C**	49.	**C**
10.	**A**	20.	**A**	30.	**A**	40.	**C**	50.	**C**

Item Classification Chart Diagnostic Test

Error	Question	See Page
Fragment	10	47, 75
Run-on	29	75
Subject-verb Agreement	2, 23, 37	76
Pronoun-Antecedent Agreement	22, 44	76
Pronoun Reference	4, 16	56
Case	11, 15, 17, 42	27, 54, 76
Unclear Placement of Modifier		
Dangling Modifier	27, 32, 33, 34	59, 77
Parallel Structure	6, 19, 28, 31, 36, 39	60, 77
Sequence of Tenses	1, 13, 14, 49	57
Mood	12, 35	58
Verb Conjugation	47	30
Transitive — Intransitive verbs	8	39
Adjective Comparison		
Adjective-Adverb Confusion	7	77
Double Negative		
Diction	5, 24, 40, 41, 46, 50	77
Idiomatic Expression	20, 43	65
No Error in Question	3, 9, 18, 21, 25, 26, 30, 38, 45, 48	

How Well Did You Do on This Diagnostic Test?

1. Find your raw score.

    a. Count the number of correct answers.

    b. Count the number of incorrect answers. (Do not count blanks as incorrect answers.)

    c. Use this formula to find your raw score:

    Raw Score = Number Correct − ¼ Number Incorrect

    Example: A student answers 41 questions correctly. He answers seven incorrectly and leaves two questions unanswered. His raw score is 41 − 1.75 (one-fourth of 7) which equals 39.25.

2. Evaluate your raw score.

Raw Score	Evaluation
45 to 50	Superior
39 to 44	Above average
33 to 38	Average
15 to 32	May need remedial work in college
Below 15	Definitely needs remedial work

How Can You Profit from This Test?

1. Look at the explanation of answers which follows this page. Notice the areas where you made your errors.

2. Chapters 3–5 of this book contain a review of the important elements of grammar, diction, style, and punctuation covered in this test. Study the sections which discuss the areas where you made your errors. If you scored low on this test, you should review all three chapters.

3. Take the tests in Part III. Find your raw score for each test and review the areas where you did poorly.

Answers Explained—Diagnostic Test

1. **C** The sequence of tenses of the verbs in the two clauses of the sentence is incorrect. Since the past tense is used in the subordinate clause, the present tense is inappropriate in the main clause. The correct verb is *refused*.

2. **B** This sentence contains an error in agreement between the subject and its verb. *Estragon* (singular) requires the singular verb *was renowned*.

3. **E** There is no error in this sentence.

4. **C** The antecedent of the pronoun *which* is vague. The sentence can be revised as follows: *The President learned of the newest snag in the negotiations to free the hostages; this made him very unhappy.*

5. **C** An error in diction occurs in this sentence. Three horses are mentioned; *former* should be used only when two things are being discussed. Use *first*.

6. **B** Parallel structure is violated in this sentence. The phrase *without fear* should be changed to *fearlessly*, to parallel the adverb *aggressively*.

7. **A** *Seemed* is a copulative verb and should be followed by a predicate adjective. Therefore, change *endlessly* to *endless*.

8. **C** Since the verb *are laying* has no object, the intransitive verb *to lie* should be used. Change *laying* to *lying*.

9. **E** All four underlined phrases are correct.

10. **A** This is an incomplete or fragment sentence. Replace the participle *talking* with a subject and verb like *Mary talked*.

11. **D** Error in case. The object of the preposition *after* should be in the objective case. Change *I* to *me*.

12. **B**   The *if* clause requires the subjunctive mood, since it is describing something that is contrary to fact. Change *would have signed* to *had signed*.

13. **C**   The rules concerning sequence of tenses are violated in this sentence. Change *opens* to *opened*.

14. **B**   This sentence also illustrates faulty sequence of tenses. Change *insists* to *insisted*.

15. **D**   Error in case. The subject of the verb should be in the nominative case. Change *me* to *I*.

16. **A**   *Which* is a relative pronoun that should be used only to refer to things. Change *which* to *who*.

17. **C**   *He* is in the wrong case. Since it is one object of the preposition *between*, use the objective pronoun *him*.

18. **E**   The sentence is correct.

19. **D**   The repetition of the verb *was* in this sentence is unnecessary. It also violates the parallel structure of the sentence, since the second phrase, *an outstanding athlete*, does not contain the verb. Delete *was*.

20. **A**   The preposition *by* should not be used to follow *enamored*. Use *of* instead.

21. **E**   The sentence is correct.

22. **B**   Error in agreement between pronoun and antecedent. *Who* refers to persons; *which*, to things. Use *which* to refer to *cat*.

23. **C**   The antecedent of *who* is *candidates*, which is a plural noun. To agree with the subject, the verb should be in the plural form. Change *is* to *are*.

24. **B**   Change *for* to *of*. This illustrates an error in diction.

25. **E**   This sentence is correct.

26. **A**   Choice (A) is best. Choice (B) is idiomatically incorrect; it would be correct if the phrase *of any* were deleted. Choices (C), (D), and (E) introduce a faulty comparison. Since John is one of the boys in the class, the word *other* is needed to correct the implication that John is taller than himself.

27. **C**   Choice (C) corrects the dangling participle which is found in the other choices.

28. **E**   Choice (E) corrects the lack of parallel structure which exists in the other choices. The infinitive *to fail* is needed to parallel *to do well*.

29. **D**   Choices (A), (B), and (E) are run-on sentences. Choice (C) changes the meaning of the sentence. Choice (D) is correct.

30. **A**   Choice (A) is best. Choice (B) changes the meaning of the sentence because it does not mention that this was the first time Maria had entered the school. Choice (C) also changes the meaning of the sentence because it does not mention the other fine qualities of the school. Choice (D) suffers from a faulty comparison, and choice (E) changes the meaning of the sentence.

31. **C**   Choice (C) corrects the lack of parallel structure found in choices (A) and (B). Choices (D) and (E) make improper use of an adverb (*comfortably*) instead of an adjective (*comfortable*).

32. **B**   Choice (B) corrects the dangling participle found in choice (A) and choice (C). Choice (D) has an error in agreement between the plural pronoun *they* and its singular antecedent *team*. Choice (E) changes the meaning of the sentence.

33. **E**   Choices (A) and (B) suffer from dangling participles. In addition, choice (A) has an error in agreement between the singular subject (*daydreaming*) and the plural verb (*enable*). Choices (C) and (D) change the meaning of the sentence.

34. **D**   Choice (A) suffers from a dangling participle. Choice (B) does not correct the error. Choice (C) is unnecessarily wordy. Choice (E) is not as clear as Choice (D); in fact, it could be taken to mean that the car was walking along the road!

35. **B**   Choices (A), (C), and (E) imply that driving a car at any speed is speeding. Choice (D) is wrong because the subjunctive mood is required in the *if* clause.

36. **D**   The use of *and* in choices (A) and (B) calls for the infinitive form of the verb *to make* in order to maintain parallel structure. Choice (C) provides the infinitive; however, the expression *make him to feel* is idiomatically incorrect. The same idiom error is found in choice (E).

37. **D**   Choices (A), (B), and (E) have an error in agreement: the plural verb *have been scheduled* should be the singular *has been scheduled* because its subject, *first*, is singular. The word *and* in choices (B) and (C) is unnecessary.

38. **A**   Choice (B) changes the meaning of the sentence. Choice (C) suffers from the needless repetition of *of*. Choice (D) violates parallel structure. Choice (E) changes the meaning of the sentence by adding the idea that the labor was *devastating*.

39. **C**   Choices (A), (B), and (D) violate parallel structure. Choice (E) is awkward and unclear.

40. **C**   *Due to* in choice (A) should not be used as a substitute for *because of*. The phrase *the reason is that* (choice C) is preferable to *the reason is because of* (choice B). Choice (E) is unnecessarily wordy.

41. **B**   *Between* should not be used when talking of more than two people or things. *Among* is the correct word.

42. **C**   Error in case. A noun or pronoun preceding a gerund should be in the possessive case. Change *Nixon* to *Nixon's*.

43. **A**   *Of* is idiomatically incorrect. Change *of* to *for*.

44. **D**   Choice (D) is an error in agreement. Change *their* to *its*, since the antecedent of the pronoun is the singular *war*.

45. **E**   This sentence is correct.

46. **C**   Error in diction. Change *altogether* to *all together*.

47. **D**   Choice (D) uses the wrong form of the irregular verb *to begin*. Change *had began* to *had begun*.

48. **E**   This sentence is correct.

49. **C**   Choice (C) contains an error in tense. Change *throws* to *threw*, to match the other past tense verb *came*.

50. **C**   Choice (C) contains an error in diction. Change *affect* to *effect*. *Affect* should never be used as a noun.

a review of standard written English

part two

chapter 3

grammar and usage: the essentials

the parts of speech

1. **Nouns** are words that name or designate persons, places, things, states, or qualities. *John Jones, Africa, book,* and *justice* are examples of nouns.

2. **Pronouns** are words used in place of nouns. *He, we, them, who, which, this, what, each, everyone,* and *myself,* are examples of pronouns.

3. **Verbs** are words or phrases which express action or state of being. *Eat, memorize, believe, feel,* and *seem* are examples of verbs.

4. **Adjectives** are words which serve as modifiers of nouns. *Famous, attractive, tall,* and *devoted* are examples of adjectives.

5. **Adverbs** are words that modify verbs, adjectives, or other adverbs. *Too, very, happily,* and *quietly* are examples of adverbs.

6. **Prepositions** are words used with nouns or pronouns to form phrases. *From, with, between, of,* and *to* are examples of prepositions.

7. **Conjunctions** are words which serve to connect words, phrases, and clauses. *And, but, when,* and *because* are examples of conjunctions.

8. **Articles** are the words *the, a,* and *an.* These words serve to identify the word they modify as a noun.

9. **Interjections** are grammatically independent words or expressions. *Alas, wow,* and *oh my* are examples of interjections.

25

Nouns

Nouns are inflected; that is, they change in form to indicate number and case. *Number* refers to the distinction between singular and plural; *case* refers to the way in which a noun is related to other elements in the sentence.

number

Nouns are either singular or plural. To form the plural form of a noun:

(1)   Add *s* to the singular.

girl / girls   house / houses

(2)   Add *es* when the noun ends in *s, x, z, ch,* or *sh.*

dish / dishes   church / churches

(3)   Add *s* when the noun ends in *o* preceded by a vowel.

folio / folios   trio / trios

(4)   Add *es* when the noun ends in *o* preceded by a consonant.

tomato / tomatoes   potato / potatoes
(Exceptions to this rule: contraltos, pianos, provisos, dynamos, Eskimos, sopranos.)

(5)   Add *s* to nouns ending in *f* or *fe* after changing these letters to *ve.*

knife / knives   shelf / shelves
(Exceptions to this rule: chiefs, dwarfs, griefs, reefs, roofs, safes, scarfs.)

(6)   Add *s* to nouns ending in *y* preceded by a vowel.

boy / boys   valley / valleys

(7)   Add *es* to nouns ending in *y* preceded by a consonant and change the *y* to *i.*

baby / babies   story / stories

(8)   Add *s* to the important part of a hyphenated word.

brother-in-law / brothers-in-law
passer-by / passers-by

(9)   Add *s* or *es* to proper nouns.

Frank / Franks   Smith / Smiths
Jones / Joneses   Charles / Charleses
(Note that the apostrophe (') is not used.)

(10)   Add *s* or *es* to either the title or the proper noun when both are mentioned.

Doctor Brown / Doctors Brown or Doctor Browns
Miss Smith / Misses Smith or Miss Smiths

(11) Add *'s* to form the plural of letters, numerals and symbols.

e / e's   9 / 9's
etc. / etc.'s   & / &'s

(12) Change to a different form in the following cases:

foot / feet   tooth / teeth
goose / geese   woman / women
louse / lice   child / children
man / men   ox / oxen

(13) Retain the foreign form with some words of foreign origin.

alumna / alumnae   focus / foci
alumnus / alumni   genus / genera
analysis / analyses   hypothesis / hypotheses
antithesis / antitheses   larva / larvae
bacillus / bacilli   matrix / matrices
bacterium / bacteria   monsieur / messieurs
basis / bases   oasis / oases
crisis / crises   parenthesis / parentheses
criterion / criteria   thesis / theses
erratum / errata   trousseau / trousseaux

Note: The correct formation or spelling of plurals is *not* directly tested on the TSWE. However, you will need to be able to recognize singular and plural noun forms in order to detect certain grammatical errors.

case

Nouns are also inflected to show possession. The possessive case of nouns is formed in the following manner:

(1) If the noun ends in *s*, add an apostrophe (').

(2) If the noun does not end in *s*, add an apostrophe (') and an *s*. Examples:

The doctor's office (The office of the doctor)
The doctors' office (The office of two or more doctors)
The girl's books (The books of one girl)
The girls' books (The books of two or more girls)

Note that in nouns of one syllable ending in *s*, either the apostrophe or the apostrophe and an *s* may be used.

James' hat and James's hat are both correct.

A noun preceding a gerund should be in the possessive case.

Incorrect: The teacher complained about John talking.
Correct: The teacher complained about John's talking.

Pronouns

Pronouns are classified as *personal, relative, interrogative, demonstrative, indefinite, intensive,* or *reflexive.*

personal pronouns

Personal pronouns indicate the person speaking, the person spoken to, or the person spoken about. They are inflected to indicate case and number. In the third person, they also indicate gender. *He* is the masculine pronoun, *she* is the feminine pronoun, and *it* is the neuter or common gender pronoun.

The *First Person*
(the person speaking or writing)

Case	Singular	Plural
Nominative	I	me
Possessive	my, mine	our, ours
Objective	me	us

The *Second Person*
(the person spoken or written to)

Case	Singular	Plural
Nominative	you	you
Possessive	your, yours	your, yours
Objective	you	you

The *Third Person*
(the person, place, or thing spoken or written about)

Third Person Masculine

Case	Singular	Plural
Nominative	he	they
Possessive	his	their, theirs
Objective	him	them

Third Person Feminine

Case	Singular	Plural
Nominative	she	they
Possessive	her, hers	their, theirs
Objective	her	them

	Third Person Neuter	
Case	*Singular*	*Plural*
Nominative	it	they
Possessive	its	their, theirs
Objective	it	them

relative pronouns

The relative pronouns are *who, which,* and *that.* They are used to relate a word in the independent clause (see the section on Clauses later in this chapter) to a dependent clause. *Who* is used to refer to persons, *which* to things, and *that* to both persons and things. Like the personal pronouns, *who* has different forms according to case:

Case	*Singular*	*Plural*
Nominative	who	who
Possessive	whose	whose
Objective	whom	whom

interrogative pronouns

The interrogative pronouns are *who, which,* and *what.* They are used to ask questions. *Which* and *what* do not change according to case. *Who* follows the forms listed above.

demonstrative pronouns

The demonstrative pronouns are *this, that, these,* and *those.* They serve to point out people, places, and things. The plural of *this* is *these;* the plural of *that* is *those.*

indefinite pronouns

The indefinite pronouns include *all, anyone, each, either, everyone, somebody, someone, whatever, whoever.* The objective case of *whoever* is *whomever;* all the other indefinite pronouns have the same form in the nominative and objective cases. The possessive case of any indefinite pronoun is formed by adding *'s: everyone's, somebody's.*

intensive and reflexive pronouns

Intensive pronouns are used to intensify or emphasize a noun or pronoun.

I <u>myself</u> did it.

Reflexive pronouns refer back to the subject of the sentence.

I taught <u>myself</u>.

The intensive and reflexive pronouns have the same singular and plural forms:

Person	Singular	Plural
First	myself	ourselves
Second	yourself	yourselves
Third	himself	themselves
	herself	themselves

some problems involving pronouns

The major grammatical problems concerning pronouns involve agreement and case. These are discussed in Chapter 4.

An intensive pronoun should not be used without the noun or pronoun to which it refers.

Incorrect: <u>Herself</u> baked the cake.
Correct: <u>Mary</u> <u>herself</u> baked the cake.

Like nouns, a pronoun preceding a gerund should be in the possessive case.

Incorrect: She objected to <u>me</u> going out too late.
Correct: She objected to <u>my</u> going out too late.

Verbs

conjugation of verbs

Verbs change their forms to indicate person, number, tense, mood, and voice. The various changes involved are indicated when the verb is *conjugated*. In order to conjugate a verb, its *principal parts* must be known. These are:

Infinitive: *to talk*
Present tense: *talk*
Present participle: *talking*
Past tense: *talked*
Past participle: *talked*

When the principal parts of a verb are listed, the infinitive and the present participle are often omitted.

CONJUGATION OF THE REGULAR VERB *TO CARRY*
(principal parts: *carry, carried, carried*)

Indicative Mood—Active Voice

Present Tense

Singular	Plural
I carry	We carry
You carry	You carry
He, she, it carries	They carry

Past Tense

Singular	Plural
I carried	We carried
You carried	You carried
He, she, it carried	They carried

Future Tense

Singular	Plural
I shall (will) carry*	We shall (will) carry*
You will carry	You will carry
He, she, it will carry	They will carry

Present Perfect Tense

Singular	Plural
I have carried	We have carried
You have carried	You have carried
He, she, it has carried	They have carried

Past Perfect Tense

Singular	Plural
I had carried	We had carried
You had carried	You had carried
He, she, it had carried	They had carried

Future Perfect Tense

Singular	Plural
I shall (will) have carried*	We shall (will) have carried*
You will have carried	You will have carried
He, she, it will have carried	They will have carried

*Some traditional grammarians assert that only the auxiliary verb *shall* is correct in the first person when simple future or future perfect meaning is intended. Most modern writers and grammarians do not accept this distinction, however, and *I will* may be regarded as equally correct.

Indicative Mood—Passive Voice

Present Tense

Singular	Plural
I am carried	We are carried
You are carried	You are carried
He, she, it is carried	They are carried

Past Tense

Singular	Plural
I was carried	We were carried
You were carried	You were carried
He, she, it was carried	They were carried

Future Tense

Singular	Plural
I shall (will) be carried*	We shall (will) be carried*
You will be carried	You will be carried
He, she, it will be carried	They will be carried

Present Perfect Tense

Singular	Plural
I have been carried	We have been carried
You have been carried	You have been carried
He, she, it has been carried	They have been carried

Past Perfect Tense

Singular	Plural
I had been carried	We had been carried
You had been carried	You had been carried
He, she, it had been carried	They had been carried

Future Perfect Tense

Singular	Plural
I shall (will) have been carried*	We shall (will) have been carried*
You will have been carried	You will have been carried
He, she, it will have been carried	They will have been carried

Subjunctive Mood—Active Voice

Present Tense

Singular	Plural
If I, you, he carry	If we, you, they carry
If I, you, he be carried	If we, you, they be carried

Past Tense

Singular	Plural
If I, you, he carried	If we, you, they carried
If I, you, he were carried	If we, you, they were carried

Subjunctive Mood—Passive Voice

Present Tense

Singular	Plural
If I, you, he be carried	If we, you, they be carried

Past Tense

Singular	Plural
If I, you, he were carried	If we, you, they were carried

Imperative Mood—Present Tense

Carry!

Note that most verbs form the past and past participle forms by adding *ed* to the present tense. Verbs ending in *y* (like *carry*) change the *y* to *i* before adding *ed*. Verbs ending in *e* (like *raise*) add *d* only.

Verbs which do not follow these rules are called *irregular*. The principal parts of the most common irregular verbs are listed below:

PRINCIPAL PARTS OF IRREGULAR VERBS

Present Tense	Past Tense	Past Participle
arise	arose	arisen
awake	awaked, awoke	awaked, awoke
bear	bore	borne
beat	beat	beaten
befall	befell	befallen
begin	began	begun
bend	bent	bent
bid (command)	bade	bidden
bid (command)	bid	bid
bind	bound	bound
blow	blew	blown
break	broke	broken
bring	brought	brought
broadcast	broadcast, broadcasted	broadcast, broadcasted
build	built	built
burst	burst	burst
buy	bought	bought

Present Tense	Past Tense	Past Participle
cast	cast	cast
catch	caught	caught
choose	chose	chosen
cling	clung	clung
come	came	come
creep	crept	crept
deal	dealt	dealt
dive	dived, dove	dived
do	did	done
draw	drew	drawn
drink	drank	drunk
drive	drove	driven
eat	ate	eaten
fall	fell	fallen
feed	fed	fed
feel	felt	felt
fight	fought	fought
find	found	found
flee	fled	fled
fling	flung	flung
fly	flew	flown
forbear	forbore	forborne
forbid	forbade	forbidden
forget	forgot	forgotten, forgot
forgive	forgave	forgiven
forsake	forsook	forsaken
freeze	froze	frozen
get	got	got, gotten
give	gave	given
go	went	gone
grow	grew	grown
hang*	hung, hanged*	hung, hanged*

*See the list of Words Often Misused in Chapter 4.

Present Tense	Past Tense	Past Participle
have	had	had
hit	hit	hit
hold	held	held
kneel	knelt, kneeled	knelt
know	knew	known
lay	laid	laid
lead	led	led
leave	left	left
lend	lent	lent
lie	lay	lain
lose	lost	lost
make	made	made
meet	met	met
put	put	put
read	read	read
ring	rang	rung
rise	rose	risen
run	ran	run
see	saw	seen
seek	sought	sought
sell	sold	sold
send	sent	sent
set	set	set
shine	shone	shone
shrink	shrank, shrunk	shrunk, shrunken
sing	sang	sung
sink	sank	sunk
slay	slew	slain
sit	sat	sat
sleep	slept	slept
slide	slid	slid
sling	slung	slung
slink	slunk	slunk
speak	spoke	spoken

Present Tense	Past Tense	Past Participle
spring	sprang, sprung	sprung
steal	stole	stolen
stick	stuck	stuck
sting	stung	stung
stride	strode	stridden
strike	struck	struck
swear	swore	sworn
sweat	sweat, sweated	sweated
sweep	swept	swept
swim	swam	swum
swing	swung	swung
take	took	taken
teach	taught	taught
tear	tore	torn
telecast	telecast, telecasted	telecast, telecasted
tell	told	told
think	thought	thought
thrive, thrived	throve, thriven	throve, thriven
throw	threw	thrown
wake	waked, woke	waked, woken
wear	wore	worn
weep	wept	wept
win	won	won
wind	wound	wound
work	worked, wrought	worked, wrought
wring	wrung	wrung
write	wrote	written

how the verb tenses are used

In addition to the six tenses listed in the typical conjugation shown above, there are *progressive* and *intensive* forms for some of the tenses. These will be discussed as we consider the uses of each tense.

The present tense indicates that the action or state being defined by the verb is occurring at the time of speaking or writing.

I <u>plan</u> to vote for the incumbent.

The present tense is used to state a general rule.

> Honesty <u>is</u> the best policy.

The present tense is used to refer to artistic works of the past or to artists of the past whose work is still in existence.

> Michelangelo <u>is</u> one of Italy's most famous artists.

The present tense is used to tell the story of a fictional work.

> In *Gone with the Wind,* Rhett Butler finally <u>realizes</u> that Scarlett O'Hara <u>is</u> unworthy of his love.

The progressive form of the present tense (a combination of the present tense of the verb *to be* and the present participle) indicates prolonged action or state of being.

> I am <u>thinking</u> about the future.
> You <u>are flirting</u> with disaster.
> He <u>is courting</u> my sister.
> We <u>are planning</u> a trip to Yosemite National Park.
> They <u>are being</u> stubborn.

The intensive form of the present tense (a combination of the verb *to do* and the infinitive) creates emphasis.

> He <u>does care</u>.
> We <u>do intend</u> to stay.

The past tense is used to indicate that an event occurred in a specific time in the past and that the event is completed.

> I <u>lived</u> in New York in 1979.
> I <u>lived</u> in that house for six years. (I no longer live there.)

The progressive form of the past tense combines the past tense of *to be* and the present participle. It indicates prolonged past action or state of being.

> I, he, she, it <u>was playing</u>.
> We, you, they <u>were going</u>.

The intensive form of the past tense combines the past tense of *to do* and the infinitive. It creates emphasis.

> I <u>did know</u> the answer to the question.

The future tense makes a statement about a future event. As indicated in the conjugation of the verb *to carry*, traditional grammarians distinguish between the use of *shall* and *will* in the future tense. According to this rule, the simple future uses *shall* in the first person and *will* in the second and third persons.

I, we shall go.

You, he, they will go.

To show determination, promise, or command, *will* is used in the first person and *shall* in the second and third persons.

I will pay this bill on Friday.

You, he, they shall comply with this order.

However, most contemporary grammarians accept the use of *shall* and *will* interchangeably in the future tense.

The progressive form of the future tense combines the future tense of *to be* and the present participle.

I shall be wearing a white jacket.

He will be going with my brother.

The present perfect tense combines the present tense of *to have* and the past participle.

I have gone.

He has eaten his breakfast.

Whereas the past tense refers to a definite time in the past, the present perfect tense indicates that the event is perfected or completed at the present time.

The present perfect tense is also used to indicate that the event began in the past and is continuing into the present.

He has attended Yale University for three years. (He is still attending Yale.)

The progressive form of the present perfect tense combines the present perfect tense of *to be* and the present participle.

He has been complaining about a pain in his side for some time.

The past perfect tense is formed by combining the past participle of the verb and the past tense of the verb *to have*. It describes an event which was completely perfected at a definite time in the past. Its major use is to indicate that one event occurred before another in the past.

By the time the firemen arrived, the boys had extinguished the blaze. (The fire was put out before the firemen came.)

The progressive form of the past perfect tense is formed by combining the present participle of the verb and the past perfect tense of *to be*.

I had been holding this package for you for three weeks.

The future perfect tense is formed by combining the past participle of the verb and the future tense of the verb *to have*. It indicates that a future event will be completed before a definite time in the future.

By one in the afternoon, he will have finished his lunch and will have returned to the office.

The progressive form of the future perfect tense is formed by combining the present participle of the verb and the future perfect tense of *to be*.

> They <u>will have been swimming</u> all afternoon.

kinds of verbs

Transitive verbs are verbs that require an object. The object is the receiver of the action.

> He hit the boy.
> (The object <u>boy</u> has been hit.)
>
> I received a letter.
> (The object <u>letter</u> has been received.)

Intransitive verbs do not require an object.

> She <u>is walking</u>.

Copulative verbs are intransitive verbs with the special quality of connecting the subject to a noun, pronoun, or adjective. The most common copulative verb is *to be*.

> Mr. Jones <u>is</u> the teacher.
>
> It <u>is</u> I.

(In these two sentences, <u>teacher</u> and <u>I</u> are called <u>predicate nominatives</u>.)

> The man <u>is</u> rich.
>
> The actress <u>is</u> beautiful.

(<u>Rich</u> and <u>beautiful</u> are <u>predicate adjectives</u>.)

Predicate nominatives and predicate adjectives are normally called predicate complements because they complete the thought of the copulative verb. The predicate nominative represents the same person or thing as the subject of the verb *to be* and is in the nominative case. Note:

> He is the <u>teacher</u>.
>
> The teacher is <u>he</u>.

The predicate adjective is connected to the subject by the copulative verb. The description, the *lame horse*, becomes a good statement or sentence when the copulative verb is used in the following:

> The horse <u>is lame</u>.

The other copulative verbs are *appear, become, feel, get, grow, look, seem, smell, sound,* and *taste*. These verbs should be followed by predicate adjectives.

> This <u>tastes</u> good.
>
> I <u>feel</u> sad.

This <u>sounds</u> too loud.

I <u>became</u> ill.

Be careful to distinguish between transitive and intransitive verbs. Words like *lie* and *lay, sit* and *set, rise* and *raise* often give students trouble.

(1) *Lie* is an intransitive verb, meaning "to rest or recline." Its principal parts are: *lie, lay, lain.*
     Lay is transitive and means "to place down." Its principal parts are: *lay, laid, laid.*

     Incorrect: I <u>lay</u> the book on the table.

     Correct: I <u>laid</u> the book on the table.

     Incorrect: Because I am tired, I am going to <u>lay</u> down.

     Correct: Because I am tired, I am going to <u>lie</u> down.

(2) *Sit* is intransitive. Its principal parts are: *sit, sat, sat.*
     Set may be either transitive or intransitive. Its principal parts are *set, set, set.*

     Incorrect: I am going to <u>sit</u> this tripod on the floor.

     Correct: I am going to <u>set</u> this tripod on the floor.

(3) *Rise,* meaning "to come up," is intransitive. Its principal parts are *rise, rose, risen.*
     Raise, meaning "to lift up," is transitive. Its principal parts are *raise, raised, raised.*

     Incorrect: The delta lowlands were in danger of being flooded when the sea <u>raised</u> by three feet.

     Correct: The delta lowlands were in danger of being flooded when the sea <u>rose</u> by three feet.

voice and mood

Voice is a characteristic of transitive verbs. In the **active voice**, the subject is the doer of the action stated by the verb, and the object of the verb is the receiver of the action. Example:

John caught the ball. (<u>John</u> is doing the catching and the <u>ball</u> is being caught.)

In the **passive voice**, the receiver of the action is the subject. The doer of the action may be identified by using a phrase beginning with *by.* Example:

The ball was caught.

The <u>ball</u> was caught <u>by John.</u>

Some writers prefer the active voice and object to the use of the passive. However, both voices have their virtues and neither should be regarded as incorrect.

It is inadvisable to switch from one voice to the other in the same sentence. Example:

Undesirable: The outfielder <u>raced</u> toward the wall and the ball <u>was caught.</u>

Preferable: The outfielder <u>raced</u> toward the wall and <u>caught</u> the ball.

Mood is used to indicate the intentions of the writer.
The **indicative mood** makes a statement or asks a question.

> I <u>wrote</u> you a letter.
>
> When <u>did</u> you <u>mail</u> it?

The **imperative mood** commands, directs, or requests.

> <u>Go</u> home!
>
> <u>Make</u> a left turn at the stop light.
>
> Please <u>talk</u> more slowly.

The **subjunctive mood** is used when the writer desires to express a wish or a condition contrary to fact.

> I wish I <u>were</u> able to go with you. (I am not able to go.)
>
> If he <u>were</u> less of a bore, people would invite him to their homes more frequently. (He is a bore.)

It is also used after a verb which expresses a command or a request.

> The governor has ordered that all pay increases <u>be</u> deferred.
>
> She demanded that he <u>leave</u> immediately.

verbals

The infinitive, present participle, and past participle are called non-finite verbs, or **verbals**. These forms of the verb cannot function as verbs without an auxiliary word or words.

> *Running* is not a verb.
>
> *Am running, have been running, shall be running* are verbs.
>
> *Broken* is not a verb.
>
> *Is broken, had been broken, may be broken* are verbs.

The infinitive (the verb preceded by *to*) is used chiefly as a noun. Occasionally, it may serve as an adjective or an adverb.

> John wants <u>to go</u> to the movies.
> (<u>To go</u> to the movies is the object of <u>wants</u>. It serves as a noun.)
>
> I have miles <u>to go</u> before I sleep.
> (<u>To go</u> modifies <u>miles</u>. It serves as an adjective.)
>
> <u>To be honest</u>, we almost lost the battle.
> (<u>To be honest</u> modifies the rest of the sentence. It serves as an adverb.)

The present participle usually serves as an adjective.

> <u>Flying</u> colors
>
> <u>Singing</u> waiters
>
> <u>Dancing</u> waters
>
> (In each case, the participle modifies the noun it precedes.)
>
> <u>Writing on the blackboard</u>, the scientist presented his arguments in favor of his thesis. (<u>Writing on the blackboard</u> is a <u>participial phrase</u> modifying <u>scientist</u>.)

The present participle may also serve as a noun. When it does so, it is called a **gerund**.

> <u>Jogging</u> is good exercise.
>
> <u>Dieting</u> to lose weight requires discipline.

A noun or pronoun preceding a gerund should be in the possessive case.

> <u>My</u> talking to Mary annoyed the teacher.
>
> We were frightened by <u>Helen's</u> fainting.

The past participle serves as an adjective.

> <u>Broken</u> homes
>
> <u>Fallen</u> arches
>
> <u>Pained</u> expressions

Adjectives

Adjectives are words which limit or describe nouns and pronouns. Examples:

> <u>Three</u> men
> The <u>fourth</u> quarter
> (<u>Three</u> and <u>fourth</u> limit the words they precede.)
>
> A <u>pretty</u> girl
> (<u>Pretty</u> describes the word it precedes.)
>
> A <u>daring</u> <u>young</u> man
> (<u>Daring</u> is a participle used as an adjective, and describes <u>man</u>; <u>young</u> describes <u>man</u>.)

Adjectives usually precede the word they limit or describe. However, for emphasis the adjective may follow the word it modifies. Example:

> One nation, <u>indivisible</u>

Adjectives are often formed from nouns by adding suffixes such as *-al, -ish, -ly,* and *-ous.*

Noun	Adjective
fiction	fictional
girl	girlish
friend	friendly
joy	joyous

Predicate adjectives are adjectives which follow the copulative verbs *be, appear, become, feel, get, grow, look, seem, smell, sound,* and *taste*. These adjectives follow the verb and refer to its subject.

> The man is <u>tall</u>. (A tall man)
>
> The lady looks <u>beautiful</u>. (A beautiful lady)

Adjectives are inflected; that is, they change form to indicate degree of comparison: *positive, comparative,* or *superlative.* The *positive degree* indicates the basic form without reference to any other object. The *comparative degree* is used to compare two objects. The *superlative degree* is used to compare three or more objects. Usually, *er* or *r* is added to the positive to form the comparative degree; *est* or *st* to form the superlative. Some adjectives of two syllables and all adjectives longer than two syllables use *more* (or *less*) to form the comparative degree and *most* (or *least*) to form the superlative. Examples:

Positive	Comparative	Superlative
tall	taller	tallest
pretty	prettier	prettiest
handsome	more handsome	most handsome
expensive	less expensive	least expensive

A few adjectives have irregular comparative and superlative forms. These include:

Positive	Comparative	Superlative
good	better	best
bad	worse	worst
ill	worse	worst

Adverbs

Adverbs are words which modify verbs, adjectives, or other adverbs. Examples:

> He spoke <u>sincerely</u>. (Sincerely modifies <u>spoke</u>.)
>
> <u>Almost</u> any person can afford this kind of vacation.
> (<u>Almost</u> modifies the adjective <u>any</u>.)
>
> He spoke <u>very</u> sincerely. (<u>Very</u> modifies the adverb <u>sincerely</u>.)

Most adverbs end in *ly* (*angrily, stupidly, honestly*). However, some adjectives also end in *ly* (*manly, womanly, holy, saintly*). Some commonly used words have the same form for the adjective and the adverb. These include *early, far, fast, hard, high, late, little, loud, quick, right, slow,* and *well.*

Adjective	Adverb
The *early* bird	He left *early*.
A *far* cry	You have gone too *far*.
He is a *fast* worker.	Don't go so *fast*.
This is *hard* to do.	He slapped him *hard*.
A *high* voice	Put it *high* on the agenda.
A *late* bloomer	He arrived *late*.
Men of *little* faith	He is a *little* late.
A *loud* explosion	He spoke *loud*.
A *quick* step	Think *quick*.
The *right* decision	Do it *right*.
A *slow* worker	Drive *slow*.
All is *well*.	He was *well* prepared.

Adverbs, like adjectives, change form to show comparison. The comparative degree uses the word *more* (or *less*); the superlative degree, the word *most* (or *least*). *Badly* and *well* have irregular comparative forms.

Positive	Comparative	Superlative
quickly	more quickly	most quickly
rapidly	less rapidly	least rapidly
badly	worse	worst
well	better	best

Prepositions

Prepositions are words which combine with nouns, pronouns and noun substantives to form phrases which act as adverbs, adjectives, or nouns.

I arrived <u>at ten o'clock</u>. (Adverbial phrase)

The man <u>with the broken arm</u>. (Adjective phrase)

The shout came from <u>outside the house</u>. (Noun phrase acting as object of <u>from</u>)

The most common prepositions are:

about	behind	during	on	to
above	below	except	out	touching
after	beneath	excepting	over	toward
against	beside	for	past	under
along	besides	from	round	underneath
amid	between	in	save	up
among	beyond	into	since	with
around	but	notwithstanding	through	within
at	by	of	throughout	without
before	down	off	till	

Some verbs call for the use of specific prepositions. See the list of Idiomatic Expressions in Chapter 4.

Conjunctions

Conjunctions are connecting words which join words, phrases and clauses. There are two kinds of conjunctions:

Coordinating conjunctions connect words, phrases, and clauses of equal rank. They are *and, but, or, nor, for, whereas,* and *yet.* Pairs of words like *either . . . or, neither . . . nor, both . . . and, not only . . . but also* are a special kind of coordinating conjunction. These are called *correlative conjunctions.*

Subordinating conjunctions connect dependent clauses to independent clauses. Some of the more common subordinating conjunctions are *although, as, because, if, since, so, than, though, till, unless, until, whether,* and *while.* Also, when the relative pronouns *who, which, that* introduce a dependent clause, they act as subordinating conjunctions.

Independent and dependent clauses are discussed in the section on Sentence Sense later in this chapter.

Articles

The three most frequently used adjectives—*a, an,* and *the*—are called **articles**. The *definite article* is *the.* The *indefinite articles* are *a* and *an. A* is used before a word beginning with a consonant sound. *An* is used before a word beginning with a vowel sound.

A bright light

An auspicious beginning

An RCA television set

A humble beginning (the h sound is pronounced)

An hour ago (the h sound is omitted)

Interjections

Interjections are words which express emotion and which have no grammatical relation to the other words in the sentence.

> Alas, I am disconsolate.
>
> Wow! This is exciting!
>
> Eureka! I have found it.

sentence sense

The ability to write complete sentences without error is characteristic of a student who has mastered standard written English. Failure to write in complete sentences is a major weakness of students whose written compositions are considered unsatisfactory.

A sentence may be defined as a group of words that contains a subject and a predicate, expresses a complete thought, and ends with a period (.), a question mark (?), or an exclamation point (!).

The sentence must contain a finite verb which makes the statement or asks the question. Examples:

> The soldiers fought a battle.
>
> Halt!
>
> Where are you going?
>
> The students have gone home.
>
> I have been thinking about your offer.
>
> Why have you been making this accusation?
>
> Who will take your place?

(The verbs in the above sentences are: *fought, halt, are going, have gone, have been thinking, have been making,* and *will take.*)

The forms of the verb which are not finite are the *infinitive,* the *participle,* and the *gerund.* These three forms cannot act as finite verbs.

clauses

A **clause** is a group of words containing a subject and a verb. There are two kinds of clauses: **Main clauses** (also called **principal** or **independent clauses**). A main clause does not modify anything; it can stand alone as a sentence. Examples:

I went to the theater.

I failed my spelling test.

A sentence containing one main clause is called a *simple sentence.*

A sentence containing two or more main clauses is called a *compound sentence.* The clauses must be connected by a coordinating conjunction or by a semicolon (;). Examples:

I went to the theater and I saw a good production of *Hamlet.*

You must pass this test, or you will be suspended from the team.

Four boys played tennis; the rest went swimming.

Subordinate clauses (also called **dependent clauses**). A subordinate clause cannot stand alone; to be a good sentence, it must always accompany a main clause. A sentence containing a main clause and one or more subordinate clauses is called a *complex sentence.* If the subordinate clause modifies a noun or pronoun, it is called an *adjective clause.* If it modifies a verb, it is an *adverb clause* or an *adverbial clause.* A clause that acts as the subject or the object of a verb or as the object of a preposition is called a *noun clause.* Examples:

The book which is on the table belongs to my sister. (The clause which is on the table is an adjective clause because it modifies the noun book.)

She quit school because she had to go to work. (The clause because she had to go to work is an adverbial clause because it modifies the verb quit.)

I asked what the teacher did. (What the teacher did is a noun clause because it is the object of the verb asked.)

Give this medal to whoever comes in first. (Whoever comes in first is a noun clause because it is the object of the preposition to.)

phrases

A **phrase** is a group of words that lacks a subject and a predicate and acts as a unit. A phrase cannot serve as a complete sentence. These are the common types of phrases:

Prepositional phrases are introduced by a preposition and act as adjectives or adverbs. Examples:

This is an overt act of war. (Of war is an adjective phrase modifying act.)

Please come at ten a.m. (At ten a.m. is an adverbial phrase modifying come.)

Participial phrases are introduced by a participle and are used as adjectives to modify nouns and pronouns. Examples:

Fighting his way through tacklers, he crossed the goal line. (Fighting his way through tacklers is a present participial phrase modifying the pronoun he.)

Sung by this gifted artist, the words were especially stirring. (Sung by this gifted artist is a past participial phrase modifying the noun words.)

Gerund phrases are introduced by a gerund and are used as nouns. Example:

Smoking cigarettes is harmful to one's health. (Smoking cigarettes is a gerund phrase used as the subject of the verb is.)

Infinitive phrases are introduced by the infinitive form of the verb, usually preceded by *to*. They are used as nouns, adjectives, and adverbs. Examples:

To win a decisive victory is our goal. (To win a decisive victory is an infinitive phrase used as the subject of the verb is.)

I have a dress to alter. (To alter is an infinitive modifying the noun dress.)

The ice is too soft to skate on. (To skate on is an infinitive modifying the adjective soft.)

Grammarians disagree about the interpretation of sentences like *I want him to buy a suit.* Some regard *him to buy a suit* as an infinitive clause with *him* the subject of the infinitive *to buy.* Others regard *him* as the object of the verb *want* and *to buy a suit* as an infinitive phrase acting as an objective complement. No matter how the sentence is interpreted, *him* is correct.

chapter 4

common problems in grammar and usage

common problems in grammar

Sentence Fragments

A **sentence fragment** occurs when a phrase or a dependent clause is incorrectly used as a sentence. Illustrations of sentence fragments and ways of correcting them follow:

When he walked into the room.

Apologizing for his behavior.

To discuss the problem amicably.

In our discussion of the problem.

Or yield to their demands.

In Illustration 1, we have a dependent clause used as a sentence. To correct, either remove the subordinating conjunction *when* or add an independent clause.

He walked into the room.

When he walked into the room, we yelled "Surprise."

In Illustration 2, we have a participial or gerund phrase used as a sentence. To correct, either change the phrase to a subject and a verb or add an independent clause.

He <u>apologized</u> for his behavior.

<u>Apologizing for his behavior</u>, he tried to atone for the embarrassment he had caused.

In Illustration 3, we have an infinitive phrase. To change this phrase to a complete sentence, either change the infinitive to a finite verb and add a subject, or add a subject and verb which will make a complete thought.

We <u>discussed</u> the problem amicably.

<u>It is advisable to discuss</u> the problem amicably.

In Illustration 4, we have a prepositional phrase. To correct this fragmentary sentence, add an independent clause to which it can relate.

We <u>failed</u> to consider the public's reaction in our discussion of the problem.

In Illustration 5, we have part of a compound predicate. To correct this, combine it with the other part of the compound predicate in a single complete sentence.

<u>We must fight this aggressive act</u> or yield to their demands.

Run-on Sentences

The run-on sentence has been given many different names by grammarians, including the *comma fault* sentence, the *comma splice* sentence, and the *fused* sentence. Examples:

The jurors examined the evidence, they found the defendant guilty.

It is very cloudy I think it is going to rain.

The *comma fault* or *comma splice* sentence may be defined as a sentence in which two independent clauses are improperly connected by a comma. The first example above is an illustration of the comma fault sentence. The *fused* sentence consists of two sentences that run together without any distinguishing punctuation. The second example above illustrates this kind of error.

Any of four methods may be used to correct run-on sentences:

(1) Use a period at the end of the first independent clause instead of a comma. Begin the second independent clause with a capital letter.

<u>The jurors examined the evidence</u>. They found the defendant guilty.

<u>It is very cloudy</u>. I think it is going to rain.

(2) Connect the two independent clauses by using a coordinating conjunction.

The jurors examined the <u>evidence, and</u> they found the defendant guilty.

It is very <u>cloudy, and</u> I think it is going to rain.

(3) Use a semicolon between two main clauses not connected by a coordinating conjunction.

The jurors examined the <u>evidence; they</u> found the defendant guilty.

It is very <u>cloudy; I</u> think it is going to rain.

(4) Use a subordinating conjunction to make one of the independent clauses dependent on the other.

<u>When</u> the jurors examined the evidence, they found the defendant guilty.

<u>Because</u> it is very cloudy, I think it is going to rain.

Problems with Agreement

Problems with agreement generally involve a violation of one of the two basic rules governing agreement.

Rule I: A verb and its subject must agree in person and number. A singular verb must have a singular subject; a plural verb must have a plural subject.

If you examine the conjugation of the verb *to carry* on pages 31–33, you will observe that this rule applies only to the present and present perfect tenses. The other tenses use the same form for each of the three persons and with both singular and plural subjects. Therefore, an error in agreement cannot occur in any tense other than the present or present perfect tense, with the exception of the verb *to be*. The past tense of this verb is:

Person	Singular	Plural
first	I was	We were
second	You were	You were
third	He, she, it was	They were

Rule I concerning agreement is simple and easy to remember. However, you should watch out for the following:

(1) The verb does *not* agree with the modifier of the subject or with a parenthetical expression introduced by *as well as, with, together with,* or a similar phrase. Examples:

The father of the children is going to work. (The subject of the singular verb <u>is going</u> is the singular noun <u>father</u>. <u>Children</u> is part of the prepositional phrase <u>of the children</u>, which modifies father.)

The pupils as well as the teacher are going to the zoo. (The subject of the plural verb <u>are going</u> is the plural noun <u>pupils</u>. <u>Teacher</u> is part of the parenthetical expression <u>as well as the teacher</u>. This parenthetical expression is <u>not</u> the subject.)

(2) A plural verb is used with a compound subject (two or more nouns or pronouns connected by *and*). Examples:

<u>John and his friends</u> <u>are going</u> camping.

<u>John and Mary</u> <u>are planning</u> a party.

However, when the compound subject can be considered as a single unit or entity, regard it as singular and follow it with a singular verb. Examples:

"Jack and Jill" is a popular nursery rhyme.

Bacon and eggs is one of the most popular breakfast dishes in America.

(3) Collective nouns like *team, committee, jury, gang, class, army,* and so on are usually regarded as singular nouns. Examples:

The team is practicing for the big game.

The Revolutionary Army was at Valley Forge.

When a collective noun is used to refer to the *individual members* of the group, it is considered a plural noun.

The jury were unable to reach a verdict. (The individual jurors could not come to a decision.)

(4) The words *billiards, economics, linguistics, mathematics, measles, mumps, news* and *physics* are considered singular nouns. Examples:

Billiards is a game of skill.

Mathematics is my most difficult subject.

(5) The words *barracks, glasses, insignia, odds, pliers, scissors, tactics, tongs, trousers,* and *wages* are considered plural nouns. Examples:

These barracks have been empty for some time.

My glasses are fogged; I cannot see clearly.

(6) The words *accoustics, ethics, gymnastics, politics,* and *statistics* are singular when they refer to specific fields of study or activity. They are plural at all other times. Examples:

Ethics is part of our Humanities program.

His ethics are questionable.

(7) Names of organizations and titles of books are singular. Examples:

"The Canterbury Tales" was written by Chaucer.

The United States now has a national debt that approaches a trillion dollars.

(8) In a sentence beginning with *there* or *here,* the subject of the verb *follows* the verb in the sentence. Examples:

There are many reasons for his failure. (Reasons is the subject of the plural verb are.)

Here is my suggestion. (Suggestion is the subject of the singular verb is.)

(9) The words *anybody, anyone, each, either, every, everyone, everybody, neither, nobody, no one,* and *someone* are regarded as singular and require a singular verb. Examples:

Anyone of the students is welcome.

Each of the songs he sang was memorable.

Either of the two choices is satisfactory.

Nobody in her classes likes her.

No one is going.

Someone in this group is a liar.

(10) The words *few, many,* and *several* are regarded as plural and require a plural verb. Examples:

Many are called, but few are chosen.

Several have already been disqualified by the lawyers.

(11) The expressions *the number* and *the variety* are regarded as singular and require a singular verb. Examples:

The number of people able to meet in this room is limited by the Fire Department.

The variety of food presented at this buffet is beyond imagination.

(12) The expressions *a number* and *a variety* are regarded as plural and require a plural verb. Examples:

A number of new cases of malaria have been reported to the Health Department.

A variety of disturbances in the neighborhood have alarmed the homeowners.

(13) *Either* and *neither* are regarded as singular (see item 9 above). However, when *either* or *neither* is coupled with *or* or *nor*, a different rule applies. In these sentences, the verb agrees with the noun or pronoun that follows the word *or* or *nor*. Examples:

Either Mary or John is eligible.

Either Mary or her sisters are mistaken.

Neither Harry nor you are eligible.

Neither you nor I was invited.

(14) When using the copulative verb *to be*, be sure to make the verb agree with the subject and not with the predicate complement.

Our greatest problem is excessive taxes.

Excessive taxes are our greatest problem.

Rule II: A pronoun must agree with its antecedent in person, number and gender. (The antecedent is the noun or pronoun to which the pronoun refers.) Example:

The detectives arrested Mrs. Brown as she entered the building. (The antecedent Mrs. Brown is a third person singular feminine noun; she is the third person singular feminine pronoun.)

Rule II concerning agreement is also easy to remember. However, watch out for these potentially troublesome points:

(1) When the antecedent is an indefinite singular pronoun (*any, anybody, anyone, each, either, every, everybody, everyone, either, no body, no one, somebody,* or *someone*), the pronoun should be singular. Examples:

Everybody on the ship went to his cabin to get his life jacket.

Neither of the girls is writing her thesis.

(2) When the antecedent is compound (two or more nouns or pronouns connected by *and*), the pronoun should be plural. Example:

Mary and Jane like their new school.

(3) When the antecedent is part of an *either ... or* or *neither ... nor* statement, the pronoun should agree with the nearer antecedent. Examples:

Either John or Henry will invite Mary to his home. (Henry is closer to his.)

Neither the seller nor the buyers have submitted their final offers. (Buyers is closer to their.)

Neither the buyers nor the seller has submitted his final offer. (Seller is closer to his.)

A special note: in some sentences, Rules I and II are combined. Example:

John is one of the boys who (is, are) trying out for the team.
(In this sentence, the antecedent of who is boys, a third person plural noun. The verb should be are because are is the third person plural verb.)

Problems with Case

Nouns and pronouns have three cases:

The nominative case indicates that the noun or pronoun is being used as the subject of a verb, or as a word in apposition to the subject, or as a predicate nominative. Examples:

John is the batter. (John is in the nominative case, since it is the subject of the verb is.)

Jane, my younger sister, attends elementary school. (Sister is in the nominative case because it is in apposition with Jane, the subject of the verb attends.)

Mrs. Brown is the teacher. (Teacher is the predicate nominative of the verb is.)

The culprit is he. (He is the predicate nominative of the verb is.)

The possessive case indicates possession. Examples:

I broke Mary's doll.

John did not do his homework.

The objective case indicates that the noun or pronoun is the object (receives the action) of a transitive verb, a verbal, or a preposition. Examples:

John hit her. (Her is the object of the verb hit.)

Practicing the violin can be boring at times. (Violin is the object of the participle practicing.)

Please come with me. (Me is the object of the preposition with.)

Some special rules concerning case:

(1)　The subject of an infinitive is in the objective case. Examples:

I want <u>him</u> to go. (<u>Him</u> is the subject of the infinitive <u>to go</u>.)

I told <u>her</u> to stop talking. (<u>Her</u> is the subject of the infinitive <u>to stop</u>.)

(2)　The predicate nominative of the infinitive *to be* is in the objective case. Example:

I want the leader to be <u>him</u>. (<u>Him</u> is the predicate complement of the infinitive <u>to be</u>.)

(3)　Nouns and pronouns used as parts of the compound subject of a verb are in the nominative case. Examples:

<u>Mary</u> and <u>he</u> are going to the party. (The two parts of the compound subject, <u>Mary and he</u>, are both in the nominative case.)

<u>John</u> and <u>we</u> are friends. (<u>John</u> and <u>we</u>, the two parts of the compound subject of the verb <u>are</u>, are both in the nominative case.)

(4)　Nouns and pronouns used as parts of the compound object of a verb, a verbal, or a preposition are in the objective case. Examples:

I met <u>Mary</u> and <u>him</u> at the party. (<u>Mary</u> and <u>him</u> are the objects of the verb <u>met</u>.)

Seeing <u>Mary</u> and <u>him</u> at the party was a treat. (<u>Mary</u> and <u>him</u> are the objects of the gerund <u>seeing</u>.)

Take the food to <u>him</u> and <u>her</u>. (<u>Him</u> and <u>her</u> are objects of the preposition <u>to</u>.)

(5)　A noun or pronoun immediately preceding a gerund is in the possessive case. Examples:

<u>John's</u> talking during the lesson was rude. (<u>John's</u> immediately precedes the gerund <u>talking</u>.)

John was afraid that <u>his</u> speaking in class would be reported to his father. (<u>His</u> immediately precedes the gerund <u>speaking</u>.)

(6)　In sentences using the conjunctions *as* or *than* to make comparisons, the clause following *as* or *than* is often truncated. Such clauses are called *elliptical clauses*. In these sentences, the case of the noun or pronouns following the conjunction is based on its use in the elliptical clause. Examples:

<u>Mary</u> is as tall as <u>he</u>. (The complete sentence is <u>Mary</u> <u>is</u> as <u>tall</u> as <u>he</u> <u>is</u> tall. The nominative case is used because <u>he</u> is the subject of the verb <u>is</u>.)

The twins are older than <u>I</u>. (The complete sentence is <u>The</u> <u>twins</u> <u>are</u> <u>older</u> <u>than</u> <u>I</u> <u>am</u> old. The nominative case is used because <u>I</u> is the subject of the verb <u>am</u>.)

(7)　The case of the relative pronouns *who, whoever,* and *whosoever* is determined by their use in the clause in which they belong. Examples:

<u>Whom</u> are you talking to? (The objective case is used because <u>whom</u> is the object of the preposition <u>to</u>.)

<u>Whom</u> did you take them to be? (The objective case is used because <u>whom</u> is the predicate complement of the infinitive <u>to be</u>.)

Give this book to whomever it belongs. (The objective case is used because whomever is the object of the preposition to.)

Give this award to whoever has earned it. (The nominative case is used because whoever is the subject of the verb has earned. In this sentence, the object of the preposition to is the noun clause whoever has earned it.)

Problems with Reference of Pronouns

Since pronouns are words used in place of nouns, the words they refer to should be clear to the reader or speaker. Vagueness or ambiguity can be avoided by observing the following rules:

(1)   The pronoun should refer to only one antecedent.

Vague: The captain asked him to polish his boots.
(Whose boots are to be polished?)

Clear: The captain said, "Polish your boots."
The captain said, "Polish my boots."

(2)   The antecedent of the pronoun should be a single noun and not a general statement. The pronouns most often affected by this rule are it, this, that, and which.

Vague: The ship was pitching and tossing in the heavy seas, and it made me seasick. (It refers to the entire clause which precedes the pronoun.)

Clear: The pitching and tossing of the ship in the heavy seas made me seasick. (Combine the two clauses in order to eliminate the pronoun.)

Clear: The ship was pitching and tossing in the heavy seas, and this motion made me seasick. (Replace the vague pronoun with a noun preceded by this, that, or which.)

Vague: When the teacher walked in the room, the students were shouting, which made her very angry. (Which refers to the entire clause rather than to a single noun.)

Clear: When the teacher walked into the room, the students' shouting angered her.

Clear: When the teacher walked into the room, the students were shouting. This lack of control angered her. (A sentence has been substituted for the vague pronoun.)

(3)   The antecedent of the pronoun should be stated, not merely implied in the sentence.

Vague: My accountant has been taking classes at law school, but he does not intend to become one. (One what?)

Clear: My accountant has been taking classes at law school, but he does not intend to become a lawyer.

Problems Involving Verbs

sequence of tenses

In this section, we will discuss five errors in tense which can occur when two or more verbs are used in the same sentence. The following are illustrations of these errors:

(1)   When I called him, he doesn't answer the phone.

(2)   At the present time, I attended John Adams High School for two years.

(3)   Our attorney already presented our proposition to the Planning Commission by the time I arrived.

(4)   I hoped to have won first prize in the contest.

(5)   We had ought to pay our respects.

In Illustration 1, we have one verb in the past tense and another in the present tense. Since the actions described by both verbs have occurred or are occurring at the same time, the tenses of the two verbs should be the same:

When I called him, he didn't answer the phone. (Both verbs are in the past tense.)

When I call him, he doesn't answer the phone. (Both verbs are in the present tense.)

Illustration 2 confuses the use of the past and present perfect tenses. As stated in the section on Verbs in Chapter 3, the past tense should be used to indicate action completed in the past. The present perfect tense should be used to indicate action begun in the past and carried into the present. The phrase *At the present time* indicates that the speaker is still attending high school. Therefore, the present perfect tense is required:

At the present time, I have attended John Adams High School for two years.

Illustration 3 exemplifies the need for the past perfect tense. Two events are mentioned in this sentence. To differentiate between the time when the attorney spoke and the time when the speaker arrived, the past perfect tense should be used for the event which occurred first:

Our attorney had already presented our proposition to the Planning Commission by the time I arrived.

Illustration 4 is an example of the use of the present and the perfect infinitive. The tense of the infinitive is determined by its relation to the principal verb. At the time specified by the principal verb, *hoped,* the speaker was still expecting *to win.* Therefore, the correct form of the sentence is:

I hoped to win first prize in the contest.

The expression *had ought* in Illustration 5 is never acceptable. *Ought* is a defective auxiliary verb. It has no other form. Thus the present and past tenses of *ought* are *ought.* The correct form of Illustration 5 is:

We ought to pay our respects.

mood

As noted on page 41, verbs are conjugated in three moods: indicative, imperative, and subjunctive. Because the subjunctive mood is the least used, many students are not aware of the uses of the subjunctive which are listed below.

The subjunctive mood is used to state a wish or a condition contrary to fact.

> I wish this party were over. (The party is not over.)
>
> If I were king, I would lower taxes. (I am not king.)
>
> If he had been elected, he would have served his full term. (He was not elected.)

The subjunctive mood is also used after a verb which expresses a command or a request.

> I insist that he pay me today. (Pay is in the subjunctive mood.)
>
> I ask that this discussion be deferred. (Be is in the subjunctive mood.)

The most common error involving the subjunctive is the following:

> If he would have known about the side effects of this medicine, he would not have prescribed it for his patients.

The expression *would have known* in the subordinate clause is incorrect. The subjunctive should be used:

> If he had known about the side effects of this medicine, he would not have prescribed it for his patients.

voice

In the active voice, the subject of the verb is the doer of the action. In the passive voice, the subject of the verb is the receiver of the action.

> Active Voice: The linebacker intercepted the pass.
>
> Passive Voice: The pass was intercepted by the linebacker.

Switching from one voice to the other within a sentence is regarded as an error in style and should be avoided.

> Poor: He likes to play chess and playing bridge is also enjoyed by him.
>
> Better: He likes to play chess and he also enjoys playing bridge.

Problems Involving Modifiers
unclear placement of modifiers

In general, adjectives, adverbs, adjective phrases, adverbial phrases, adjective clauses, and adverbial clauses should be placed close to the word they modify. If these modifiers are separated from the word they modify, confusion may result. Some specific rules to apply:

(1) The adverbs *only, almost, even, ever, just, merely,* and *scarcely* should be placed next to the word they modify.

Ambiguous: I <u>almost</u> ate the whole cake. (Did the speaker eat any of the cake?)

Clear: I ate <u>almost</u> the whole cake.

Ambiguous: This house <u>only</u> cost $42,000.

Clear: <u>Only</u> this house cost $42,000. (One house was sold at this price.)

Clear: This house cost <u>only</u> $42,000. (The price mentioned is considered low.)

(2) Phrases should be placed close to the word they modify.

Unclear: The advertisement stated that a table was wanted by an elderly gentleman with <u>wooden legs</u>. (It is obvious that the advertisement was not written to disclose the gentleman's infirmity.)

Clear: The advertisement stated that a table <u>with</u> <u>wooden</u> <u>legs</u> was wanted by an elderly gentleman.

(3) Adjective clauses should be placed near the words they modify.

Misplaced: I bought groceries at the Safeway store <u>which</u> <u>cost</u> <u>$29.47</u>.

Clear: I bought groceries <u>which</u> <u>cost</u> <u>$29.47</u> at the Safeway store.

(4) Words that may modify either a preceding or following word are called *squinting modifiers*. In order to correct the ambiguity, move the modifier so that its relationship to only one word is clear.

Squinting: He said that if we refused to leave <u>in</u> <u>two</u> <u>minutes</u> he would call the police.

Clear: He said that he would call the police if we refused to leave <u>in</u> <u>two</u> <u>minutes</u>.

Clear: He said that he would call the police <u>in</u> <u>two</u> <u>minutes</u> if we refused to leave.

Squinting: We agreed <u>on</u> <u>Tuesday</u> to visit him.

Clear: <u>On</u> <u>Tuesday</u>, we agreed to visit him.

Clear: We agreed to visit him <u>on</u> <u>Tuesday</u>.

dangling modifiers

When modifying phrases or clauses precede the main clause of the sentence, good usage requires that they come directly before the subject of the main clause and clearly refer to the subject. Phrases and clauses which do not meet these requirements are called *dangling modifiers*. They seem to refer to a wrong word in the sentence, often with humorous or misleading results.

Dangling participle: Walking through Central Park, the Metropolitan Museum of Art was seen. (Is the museum walking?)

Corrected: Walking through Central Park, the tourists saw the Metropolitan Museum of Art. (The participle <u>walking</u> immediately precedes the subject of the main clause <u>tourists</u>.)

Dangling gerund phrase: Upon hearing the report that a bomb had been placed in the auditorium, the building was cleared. (Who heard the report?)

Corrected: Upon hearing the report that a bomb had been placed in the auditorium, the police cleared the building.

Dangling infinitive phrase: To make a soufflé, eggs must be broken. (Do eggs make a soufflé?)

Corrected: To make a soufflé, you have to break some eggs.

Dangling elliptical construction: When about to graduate from elementary school, the teacher talked about the problems and joys of junior high school. (Is the teacher graduating?)

Corrected: When we were about to graduate from elementary school, the teacher talked about the problems and joys of junior high school.

Problems with Parallel Structure

Balance in a sentence is obtained when two or more similar ideas are presented in *parallel form*. A noun is matched with a noun, an active verb with an active verb, an adjective with an adjective, a phrase with a phrase. A lack of parallelism weakens the sentence.

Not parallel: We are studying mathematics, French, and how to write creatively.

Parallel: We are studying mathematics, French, and creative writing. (All the objects of the verb are studying are nouns.)

Not parallel: He told the students to register in his course, to study for the examination, and that they should take the test at the end of January.

Parallel: He told the students to register in his course, to study for the examination, and to take the test at the end of January. (The parallel elements are all infinitives.)

Not parallel: The children ate all the candy and the birthday cake was devoured. (The use of the active voice in the first clause and the passive voice in the second clause creates a lack of parallelism.)

Parallel: The children ate all the candy and devoured the birthday cake. (The change in voice has been eliminated. The two verbs ate and devoured are both in the active voice.)

common problems in usage

Words Often Misused or Confused

Errors in *diction*—that is, choice of words—are often tested on the TSWE. Here are some of the most common diction errors to watch for.

accept/except. These two words are often confused. *Accept* means to receive; *except,* when used as a verb, means to preclude or exclude. *Except* may also be used as a preposition or a conjunction.

> I will <u>accept</u> the award in his absence.

> He <u>was excepted</u> from receiving the award because of his record of excessive lateness.

affect/effect. *Affect* is a verb meaning to feign or assume. *Effect,* as a verb, means to cause or bring about; as a noun, *effect* means result.

> To cover his embarrassment, he <u>affected</u> an air of nonchalance.

> As he assumed office, the newly elected governor promised to <u>effect</u> many needed reforms in the tax structure.

> What will be the <u>effect</u> of all this discussion?

aggravate. *Aggravate* means to worsen. It should not be used as a synonym for *annoy* or *irritate.*

> You will <u>aggravate</u> your condition if you try to lift heavy weights so soon after your operation.

> The teacher was irritated [not <u>aggravated</u>] by the whispering in the room.

ain't. *Ain't* is nonstandard and should be avoided.

all the farther/all the faster. These are colloquial and regional expressions and so are considered inappropriate in standard English. Use *as far as* or *as fast as* instead.

already/all ready. These expressions are frequently confused. *Already* means previously; *all ready* means completely prepared.

> I had <u>already</u> written to him.

> The students felt that they were <u>all ready</u> for the examination.

alright. *All right* should be used instead of the misspelling *alright.*

altogether/all together. *All together* means as a group. *Altogether* means entirely, completely.

> The teacher waited until the students were <u>all together</u> in the hall before she dismissed them.

> There is <u>altogether</u> too much noise in the room.

among/between. *Among* is used when more than two persons or things are being discussed; *between,* when only two persons or things are involved.

> The loot was divided <u>among</u> the three robbers.

> This is <u>between</u> you and me.

amount/number. *Amount* should be used when referring to mass, bulk, or quantity. *Number* should be used when the quantity can be counted.

I have a large <u>amount</u> of work to do.

A large <u>number</u> of books were destroyed in the fire.

and etc. The *and* is unnecessary.

being as/being that. These phrases are nonstandard and should be avoided. Use *since* or *that*.

beside/besides. These words are often confused. *Beside* means alongside of; *besides* means in addition to.

Park your car <u>beside</u> mine.

Who will be at the party <u>besides</u> Mary and John?

between. See *among*.

but what. This phrase should be avoided. Use *that* instead.

Wrong: I cannot believe <u>but what</u> he will not come.

Better: I cannot believe <u>that</u> he will not come.

can't hardly. This phrase is a double negative that borders on the illiterate. Use *can hardly*.

complected. This word is nonstandard and should be avoided. Use *complexioned*.

continual/continuous. These words are used interchangeably by many writers; however, the careful stylist should make the distinction between the two words. *Continual* refers to a sequence that is steady but interrupted from time to time. A child's crying is *continual* because it does stop crying from time to time to catch its breath or to eat or sleep. *Continuous* refers to a passage of time or space that continues uninterruptedly. The roar of the surf at the beach is *continuous*.

could of. This phrase is nonstandard. Use *could have*.

different from/different than. Contemporary usage accepts both forms; however, *different from* remains the preferred choice.

effect. See *affect*.

except. See *accept*.

farther/further. *Farther* should be used when discussing physical or spatial distances; *further*, when discussing quantities.

We have six miles <u>farther</u> to go.

<u>Further</u> discussion will be futile.

fewer/less. *Fewer* should be used with things that can be counted; *less*, with things that are not counted but measured in other ways.

There are <u>fewer</u> pupils in this class than in the other group. (Note that you can count pupils—one pupil, two pupils, and so on.)

You should devote <u>less</u> attention to athletics and more to your studies.

former/latter. Use *former* and *latter* only when you are discussing a series of two. *Former* refers to the first item of the series and *latter* to the second. If you discuss a series of three or more, use *first* and *last*.

> Both Judy and Charles are qualified for the position, but I will vote for the former.

> Sam, Bob, and Harry invited Mary to the dance, but she decided to go with the first.

further. See *farther*.

had of. This phrase is nonstandard. Use *had*.

hanged/hung. Both words are the past participle of the verb *hang*. However, *hanged* should be used when the execution of a person is being discussed; *hung* when the suspension of an object is discussed.

> The convicted murderer was scheduled to be hanged at noon.

> When the abstract painting was first exhibited, very few noticed that it had been hung upside down.

healthful/healthy. These two words should not be confused. *Healthful* describes things or conditions that provide health. *Healthy* means in a state of health.

> You should eat healthful foods like fresh vegetables, instead of the candy you have just bought.

> To be healthy, you need good food, fresh air and sunshine, and plenty of sleep.

imply/infer. These are not synonyms. *Imply* means to suggest or indicate. *Infer* means to draw a conclusion.

> Your statement implies that you are convinced of his guilt.

> Do not infer from my action in this matter that I will always be this lenient.

in back of. Avoid this expression. Use *behind* in its place.

irregardless. This is nonstandard. Use *regardless* instead.

kind of/sort of. These phrases should not be used as adverbs. Use words like *quite*, *rather*, or *somewhat* instead.

> Undesirable: I was kind of annoyed by her statement.

> Preferable: I was quite annoyed by her statement.

last/latter. See *former*.

lay/lie. *Lay*, a transitive verb, means to place; *lie*, an intransitive verb, means to rest or recline. One way of determining whether to use *lay* or *lie* is to examine the sentence. If the verb has an object, use the correct form of *lay*. If the verb has no object, use *lie*.

> He laid the book on the table. (Book is the object of the verb. The past tense of lay is correct.)

> He has lain motionless for an hour. (The verb has no object. The present perfect tense of lie is correct.)

learn/teach. *Learn* means to get knowledge; *teach* to impart information or knowledge.

> I <u>learned</u> my lesson.

> She <u>taught</u> me a valuable lesson.

leave/let. *Leave* means to depart; *let*, to permit.

> Incorrect: <u>Leave</u> me go.

> Correct: <u>Let</u> me go.

less. See *fewer*.

liable/likely. *Likely* is an expression of probability. *Liable* adds a sense of possible harm or misfortune.

> Incorrect: He is <u>liable</u> to hear you.

> Correct: He is <u>likely</u> to hear you.

> Incorrect: The boy is <u>likely</u> to fall and hurt himself.

> Correct: The boy is <u>liable</u> to fall and hurt himself.

lie. See *lay*.

mad/angry. These are not synonyms. Mad means *insane*.

number. See *amount*.

of. Don't substitute *of* for *have* in the expressions *could have*, *should have*, *must have*, and so on.

off of. The *of* is superfluous and should be deleted.

> Incorrect: I fell <u>off</u> of the ladder.

> Correct: I fell <u>off</u> the ladder.

prefer. This verb should not be followed by *than*. Use *to, before*, or *above* instead.

> Incorrect: I prefer chocolate <u>than</u> vanilla.

> Correct: I prefer chocolate <u>to</u> vanilla.

principal/principle. *Principal*, meaning chief, is mainly an adjective. *Principle*, meaning a basic law, is a noun. In a few cases, *principal* is used as a noun because the noun it once modified has been dropped. Examples:

> <u>principal</u> of a school (Originally, the <u>principal</u> teacher.)

> <u>principal</u> in a bank (Originally, the <u>principal</u> sum.)

> a <u>principal</u> in a transaction (Originally, the <u>principal</u> person.)

raise/rise. *Raise* is a transitive verb; *rise* is intransitive.

> Incorrect: They <u>are</u> <u>rising</u> the prices.

> Correct: They <u>are</u> <u>raising</u> the prices.

Incorrect: The sun <u>will</u> <u>raise</u> at 6:22 a.m.

Correct: The sun <u>will</u> <u>rise</u> at 6:22 a.m.

real. This word is an adjective and should not be used as an adverb.

Incorrect: This is a <u>real</u> good story.

Correct: This is a <u>really</u> [or <u>very</u>] good story.

the reason is because. This expression is illogical. The phrase *the reason is* should be followed by a statement of the reason.

Incorrect: <u>The</u> <u>reason</u> I was late <u>is</u> <u>because</u> there was a traffic jam.

Correct: <u>The</u> <u>reason</u> I was late <u>is</u> <u>that</u> there was a traffic jam.

same. Do not use *same* as a pronoun. Use *it, them, this, that* in its place.

Incorrect: I have received your letter of inquiry; I will answer <u>same</u> as soon as possible.

Correct: I have received your letter of inquiry; I will answer <u>it</u> as soon as possible.

sort of. See *kind of.*

teach. See *learn.*

try and. This phrase should be avoided. Use *try to* in its place.

Incorrect: I will <u>try</u> <u>and</u> find your book.

Correct: I will <u>try</u> <u>to</u> find your book.

unique. This adjective should not be qualified by *more, most, less,* or *least.*

Incorrect: This was a <u>most</u> <u>unique</u> experience.

Correct: This was a <u>unique</u> experience.

Idiomatic Expressions

An idiom is a form of expression peculiar to a particular language. Occasionally, idioms seem to violate grammatical rules; however, the common use of these expressions has made them acceptable. Some of the most common idioms in English involve prepositions. The list below indicates which preposition is idiomatically correct after the following words:

accede to	**appetite for**
accuse of	**appreciation of**
addicted to	**aside from**
adhere to	**associate with**
agreeable to	**blame for**
amazement at	**capable of**

characterized by	negligent of
compatible with	oblivious to
conversant with	observant of
desire for	partial to
desirous of	peculiar to
desist from	preview of
different from	prior to
disagree with	prone to
disdain for	revel in
dissent from	separate from
distaste for	suspect of
enveloped in	tamper with
expert in	try to
frugal of	void of
hint at	weary of
implicit in	willing to

chapter 5

punctuation for sentence sense

Few questions on the TSWE directly test your knowledge of punctuation. However, understanding the effects of various punctuation marks on the meaning and structure of a sentence is likely to be helpful on many of the questions. In this chapter, we will review the most commonly used punctuation marks and illustrate the ways they should be used.

end punctuation

The Period (.)

(1) The period is used to indicate the end of a declarative or imperative sentence.

I am going home.

Go home.

(2) It is used after initials and abbreviations.

Mr. J. C. Smith

John Rose, M.D.

(3) It is *not* used after contractions, initials of governmental agencies, chemical symbols, or radio and television call letters.

can't	didn't
IRS	FBI
HCl	Sn
WNBC	KPIX

(4) A series of three periods is used to indicate the fact that material has been omitted from a quotation.

We, the People of the United States, in Order to form a more perfect union, ... do ordain and establish this Constitution for the United States of America.

The Question Mark (?)

(1) The question mark is used after a direct question.

Who is going with you?

(2) The question mark should *not* be used when questions appear in indirect discourse.

He asked whether you would go with him.

(3) The question mark should *not* be used when a polite or formal request is made.

Will you please come with me.

(4) The question mark should *not* be used when the question is purely rhetorical.
That's very good, don't you think.

middle punctuation

The Comma (,)

(1) The comma is used to set off nouns in direct address.

Mr. Smith, please answer this question.

Tom, come here.

(2)   It is used to set off words or phrases in apposition.

Mr. Brown, our newly elected sheriff, has promised to enforce the law vigorously.

Dr. Alexander, my instructor, has written several authoritative books on this topic.

(3)   It is used to set off items in a series.

I bought milk, eggs, apples, and bread at the store.

Maine, Vermont, New Hampshire, Massachusetts, Rhode Island, and Connecticut are the states which make up New England.

The river tumbles down lofty mountains, cuts through miles of prairie land, and finally empties into the Atlantic Ocean.

(4)   The comma is used to separate the clauses of a compound sentence connected by a coordinating conjunction.

The bill to reduce taxes was introduced by Congressman Jones, and it was referred to the House Ways and Means Committee for consideration. (Note that the omission of the conjunction and would result in a run-on sentence.)

(5)   The comma is used to set off long introductory phrases and clauses that precede the main clause.

In a conciliatory speech to the striking employees, Mr. Brown agreed to meet with their leaders and to consider their complaints.

Because I was ignorant of the facts in this matter, I was unable to reach a decision.

(6)   It is used to set off unimportant (or *non-restrictive*) phrases and clauses in a sentence.

My brother, who is a physician, has invited me to spend Christmas week with him.

(7)   The comma is used to set off parenthetical words like *first, therefore, however,* and *moreover,* from the rest of the sentence.

I am, therefore, going to sue you in small claims court.

More than two inches of rain fell last week; however, this was not enough to fill our reservoirs.

(8)   It is used to set off contrasting, interdependent expressions.

The bigger they are, the harder they fall.

(9)   The comma is used to separate adjectives that could be connected by *and*.

He spoke in a kind, soothing voice.

(10)   In sentences containing direct quotations, the comma is used to separate introductory words from quoted words.

Mary said, "I hope you will understand my reasons for doing this to you."

(11)   The comma may be used to indicate omitted words whose repetition is understood.

Tall and short are antonyms; rapid and swift, synonyms.

(12)   The comma is used to separate items in dates, addresses, and geographical names.

        January 5, 1981

        Detroit, Michigan

        My address is 5225 East 28 Street, Brooklyn, New York.

(13)   The comma is used to follow the salutation in a friendly letter.

        Dear Mary,

(14)   The comma follows the complimentary close in business and friendly letters.

        Yours sincerely,

        Truly yours,

        Cordially,

The Semicolon (;)

(1)   The semicolon is used as a substitute for the comma followed by *and* that connects two independent clauses in a compound sentence.

        Mary won first prize in the contest, and John came in second.

        Mary won first prize in the contest; John came in second.

(2)   The semicolon is used before *namely, for instance,* and *for example* when they introduce a list.

        Four students were chosen to act as a committee; namely, John, Henry, Frank, and William.

(3)   When the words *however, nevertheless, furthermore, moreover,* and *therefore* are used to connect two independent clauses, they should be preceded by a semicolon.

        He worked diligently for the award; however, he did not receive it.

(4)   The semicolon is used to separate items in a list when the items themselves contain commas.

        Among the contributors to the book were Roy O. Billett, Boston University; Lawrence D. Brennan, New York University; Allan Danzig, Lafayette College; and Mario Pei, Columbia University.

The Colon (:)

(1)   The colon is used to introduce a list, especially after the words *following* and *as follows.*

On this tour, you will visit the following countries: England, France, Spain, Italy, Greece, and Israel.

(2)   The colon is used after the salutation in business letters.

Dear Sir:

Dear Dr. Brown:

To Whom It May Concern:

(3)   The colon is used when time is indicated in figures.

Please meet me at 3:30 p.m.

(4)   The colon is used to indicate ratios.

2:5 : : 6:15

Quotation Marks (" ")

(1)   Quotation marks are used to indicate the exact words of a speaker or writer. The introductory words are separated from the quotation by a comma or commas.

Patrick Henry said, "Give me liberty or give me death."

"Give me liberty," Patrick Henry said, "or give me death."

"Give me liberty or give me death," Patrick Henry said.

(2)   When quotation marks are used, the capitalization of the original quotation should be retained.

"I have always wanted," John said, "to ride a ten-speed bike." (A small t is used because to was not capitalized in the statement being quoted.)

(3)   If the quotation is a question, the question mark should appear inside the quotation marks.

John asked, "When does the party start?"

"When does the party start?" John asked.

five practice tests

part three

chapter 6

final review and test-taking suggestions

Now that you have taken the Diagnostic Test in Part I and have checked your errors by studying the Review of Standard Written English in Part II, you are ready to take the practice tests in this section of the book. Here are a few suggestions to make your work more profitable:

Limit yourself to thirty minutes for each test.

Use the answer grids provided in the book.

Remember that a penalty for guessing is assessed on the TSWE as well as on the other parts of the SAT. Guess only when you can eliminate one or more of the choices. On most items, you will probably be able to eliminate at least one of the choices.

As you take each test, remember to watch for *The Dirty Dozen*. These are the twelve most common errors in grammar and usage appearing on the TSWE. They make up a majority of the errors you will need to recognize on the exam. Here is a summary of the Dirty Dozen to review before you begin the practice tests.

the dirty dozen

1. The Run-on Sentence

Mary's party was very exciting, it lasted until two a.m. No error
‾‾‾‾ A   ‾‾‾‾ B ‾‾‾‾‾‾‾ C   ‾‾‾‾‾‾ D   ‾‾‾‾‾‾‾‾ E

The comma in choice (C) is incorrectly used and creates a run-on sentence. One way of correcting this error would be to change the comma in choice (C) to a semicolon.

2. The Sentence Fragment

Since John's talking in class was a disturbing factor. No error
‾‾‾‾‾ A ‾‾‾‾‾ B   ‾‾‾‾ C ‾‾‾‾‾‾‾‾‾‾ D   ‾‾‾‾‾‾‾‾ E

This group of words is an incomplete sentence. The deletion of choice (A) *Since* would make the group of words a complete sentence.

3. Error in the Case of a Noun or Pronoun

Let <u>us</u> keep <u>this</u> discussion about <u>my</u> salary as a salesman between you and <u>I</u>.
$\quad$ A $\qquad$ B $\qquad\qquad$ C $\qquad\qquad\qquad\qquad\qquad\qquad$ D

<u>No error</u>
$\quad$ E

The case of the pronoun in choice (D) is incorrect. Since it is the object of the preposition *between*, the pronoun should be the objective case pronoun *me*.

4. Error in Agreement between Subject and Verb

The coach along <u>with</u> the team <u>are flying</u> home <u>after</u> the victory over <u>our</u> traditional
$\qquad\qquad\quad$ A $\qquad\qquad$ B $\qquad\qquad$ C $\qquad\qquad\qquad$ D

rival. <u>No error</u>
$\qquad$ E

The verb in this sentence (*are flying*) is plural; its subject (*coach*) is singular. To correct this error in agreement, you would have to change choice (B) to *is flying*.

5. Error in Agreement between a Pronoun and its Antecedent

Every one <u>of the girls</u> <u>in the class</u> <u>is trying</u> to do <u>their</u> best. <u>No error</u>
$\qquad\quad$ A $\qquad\qquad$ B $\qquad\qquad$ C $\qquad\qquad$ D $\qquad\qquad$ E

The antecedent of the pronoun *their* (plural) is *one* (singular). To correct the error in agreement, change *their* to *her*.

6. Error in the Tense of the Verb

<u>After</u> the sun <u>set</u> behind the mountain, a cool breeze <u>sprang up</u> and brought us
$\quad$ A $\qquad\qquad$ B $\qquad\qquad\qquad\qquad\qquad\qquad$ C

welcome <u>relief from</u> the oppressive heat. <u>No error</u>
$\qquad\qquad$ D $\qquad\qquad\qquad\qquad\qquad$ E

The past perfect tense should be used in the subordinate clause, to indicate that the sun had set before the breeze sprang up. Change *set* to *had set*.

7. Failure to Use the Subjunctive Mood When Required

If I <u>was</u> your parent, I <u>would take away</u> all your privileges for <u>at least</u> a month for
$\qquad$ A $\qquad\qquad\qquad$ B $\qquad\qquad\qquad\qquad\qquad$ C

<u>your</u> part in this escapade. <u>No error</u>
$\quad$ D $\qquad\qquad\qquad\qquad$ E

A condition contrary to fact requires the subjunctive mood. Since *I* am not *your parent*, the *if* clause is describing a condition contrary to fact. Therefore, the verb should be in the subjunctive mood. Change *was* to *were* in choice (A).

8. Error in the Comparison of Adjectives

I have a <u>choice</u> of a Carribean cruise or a one-week trip to <u>California</u>; I wonder
$\qquad\qquad$ A $\qquad\qquad\qquad\qquad\qquad\qquad\qquad\qquad\qquad$ B

<u>which</u> <u>is best</u>. <u>No error</u>
$\quad$ C $\quad$ D $\qquad$ E

When comparing two things, use the comparative form of the adjective. Change *best* to *better* in choice (D).

9. Confusion in the Use of Adjectives and Adverbs

The <u>members</u> of the union felt very <u>badly</u> about the <u>President's</u> actions in
  A   B   C
<u>suppressing</u> their strike. <u>No error</u>
  D   E

A copulative verb like *feel* should be followed by a predicate adjective, not an adverb. Change *badly* to *bad* in choice (B).

10. Use of Dangling Modifiers

<u>Reaching</u> for the book, the ladder on <u>which</u> he <u>stood</u> slipped out from under <u>him</u>.
  A   B   C   D
<u>No error</u>
  E

Reaching is a dangling participle because it has nothing to modify in this sentence. Change *reaching* in choice (A) to *when he reached*.

11. Lack of Parallel Structure

In <u>this</u> book on winter sports, the author <u>discusses</u> ice-skating, <u>skiing</u>, hockey, and
  A   B   C
<u>how to fish</u> in an ice-covered lake. <u>No error</u>
  D   E

The phrase *how to fish* does not match the grammatical form of the other objects of the verb *discusses*, which are gerunds. Change *how to fish* in choice (D) to *fishing*.

12. Error in Diction or Idiom

I <u>implied</u> from his letters that he was <u>unhappy</u> about the situation <u>into</u> which he
  A   B   C
<u>had been forced</u> through no fault of his own. <u>No error</u>
  D   E

Imply, meaning hint or suggest, is incorrectly used in this sentence. Change *implied* in choice (A) to *inferred*.

hints on handling the sentence correction question

Let's start with an example:

We are going to the party <u>with Henry and the Jones's</u>.

   (A) with Henry and the Jones's
   (B) with Henry and the Joneses
   (C) with Henry and the Jones'
   (D) with the Joneses or Henry
   (E) with Henry and the Joneses son

As we examine this question looking for examples of the Dirty Dozen, we see that we may have an error in the case of the two nouns which are the object of the preposition *with*. *Henry* is correctly in the objective case, but *Jones's* is in the possessive case.

Now that we have discovered the error, we may examine the choices. Choice (A), of course, is incorrect because it repeats the original statement. Note that whenever an error exists in the original sentence, it is *not necessary* to spend time reading choice (A). Skip it and go on.

Choice (C) is incorrect for the same reason that eliminates Choice (A): *Jones'* is the correct alternate form of the possessive case of *Jones*. In Choice (E) , we have a variation of the original error. We now have two nouns that are the objects of the preposition *with—Henry* and *son*. However, we now have a different error. The case of *Joneses* is incorrect. It should be in the possessive case, either *Jones's* or *Jones'*.

Thus, we are left with Choices (B) and (D), both of which have the correct case of the two nouns. Choice (D) should be eliminated because the use of *or* in place of *and* changes the meaning of the sentence. Therefore, Choice (B) is correct.

Note that Sentence Correction questions are often best handled according to the process of elimination we've just illustrated. First eliminate any answer which repeats an error found in the original sentence. Then eliminate any answer which introduces a new error. The remaining answer must be the correct one.

other test-taking pointers

(1) On Usage questions, if the sentence contains no error, you will choose (E), which is marked as *No error* for each question. On Sentence Correction questions, however, Choice (A) should be selected if the underlined portion of the question is correct. Do not confuse the two kinds of questions.

(2) Remember that some of the fifty questions on the TSWE have no error. Do not spend too much time on any one question looking for obscure errors. On the average, from eight to twelve questions in the test will contain no grammatical errors.

(3) Remember that you need to work rapidly to complete all fifty questions in the allotted time. You may wish to save the fifteen Sentence Completion questions to do last. Since the Usage questions involve less reading, they can usually be answered more quickly. Therefore, you will have a better chance of completing more questions if you work through all the Usage questions first.

answer sheet–typical test a

To the student:

Take the following test under examination conditions.

Have on hand a supply of #2 pencils and a good eraser.

Limit yourself to thirty minutes.

Because you will be penalized for wrong answers, do not guess wildly. However, if you can eliminate some of the choices, you can improve your score by guessing.

The answer grid below is provided for your convenience. Fill in the oval which contains the letter of your choice. You may remove this page from the book for ease in marking your answers.

1. Ⓐ Ⓑ Ⓒ Ⓓ Ⓔ   14. Ⓐ Ⓑ Ⓒ Ⓓ Ⓔ   27. Ⓐ Ⓑ Ⓒ Ⓓ Ⓔ   40. Ⓐ Ⓑ Ⓒ Ⓓ Ⓔ
2. Ⓐ Ⓑ Ⓒ Ⓓ Ⓔ   15. Ⓐ Ⓑ Ⓒ Ⓓ Ⓔ   28. Ⓐ Ⓑ Ⓒ Ⓓ Ⓔ   41. Ⓐ Ⓑ Ⓒ Ⓓ Ⓔ
3. Ⓐ Ⓑ Ⓒ Ⓓ Ⓔ   16. Ⓐ Ⓑ Ⓒ Ⓓ Ⓔ   29. Ⓐ Ⓑ Ⓒ Ⓓ Ⓔ   42. Ⓐ Ⓑ Ⓒ Ⓓ Ⓔ
4. Ⓐ Ⓑ Ⓒ Ⓓ Ⓔ   17. Ⓐ Ⓑ Ⓒ Ⓓ Ⓔ   30. Ⓐ Ⓑ Ⓒ Ⓓ Ⓔ   43. Ⓐ Ⓑ Ⓒ Ⓓ Ⓔ
5. Ⓐ Ⓑ Ⓒ Ⓓ Ⓔ   18. Ⓐ Ⓑ Ⓒ Ⓓ Ⓔ   31. Ⓐ Ⓑ Ⓒ Ⓓ Ⓔ   44. Ⓐ Ⓑ Ⓒ Ⓓ Ⓔ
6. Ⓐ Ⓑ Ⓒ Ⓓ Ⓔ   19. Ⓐ Ⓑ Ⓒ Ⓓ Ⓔ   32. Ⓐ Ⓑ Ⓒ Ⓓ Ⓔ   45. Ⓐ Ⓑ Ⓒ Ⓓ Ⓔ
7. Ⓐ Ⓑ Ⓒ Ⓓ Ⓔ   20. Ⓐ Ⓑ Ⓒ Ⓓ Ⓔ   33. Ⓐ Ⓑ Ⓒ Ⓓ Ⓔ   46. Ⓐ Ⓑ Ⓒ Ⓓ Ⓔ
8. Ⓐ Ⓑ Ⓒ Ⓓ Ⓔ   21. Ⓐ Ⓑ Ⓒ Ⓓ Ⓔ   34. Ⓐ Ⓑ Ⓒ Ⓓ Ⓔ   47. Ⓐ Ⓑ Ⓒ Ⓓ Ⓔ
9. Ⓐ Ⓑ Ⓒ Ⓓ Ⓔ   22. Ⓐ Ⓑ Ⓒ Ⓓ Ⓔ   35. Ⓐ Ⓑ Ⓒ Ⓓ Ⓔ   48. Ⓐ Ⓑ Ⓒ Ⓓ Ⓔ
10. Ⓐ Ⓑ Ⓒ Ⓓ Ⓔ   23. Ⓐ Ⓑ Ⓒ Ⓓ Ⓔ   36. Ⓐ Ⓑ Ⓒ Ⓓ Ⓔ   49. Ⓐ Ⓑ Ⓒ Ⓓ Ⓔ
11. Ⓐ Ⓑ Ⓒ Ⓓ Ⓔ   24. Ⓐ Ⓑ Ⓒ Ⓓ Ⓔ   37. Ⓐ Ⓑ Ⓒ Ⓓ Ⓔ   50. Ⓐ Ⓑ Ⓒ Ⓓ Ⓔ
12. Ⓐ Ⓑ Ⓒ Ⓓ Ⓔ   25. Ⓐ Ⓑ Ⓒ Ⓓ Ⓔ   38. Ⓐ Ⓑ Ⓒ Ⓓ Ⓔ
13. Ⓐ Ⓑ Ⓒ Ⓓ Ⓔ   26. Ⓐ Ⓑ Ⓒ Ⓓ Ⓔ   39. Ⓐ Ⓑ Ⓒ Ⓓ Ⓔ

chapter 7

typical test a

Directions: In each of the sentences below, there are four underlined words or phrases. If you think there is an error in usage, grammar, diction, or punctuation in one of the underlined parts, write the letter indicated on your answer paper. If there is no error in any of the underlined parts, mark (E) on your answer paper.

> **Example:** The aircraft carrier with all her accompanying ships are going to sail to the
>   A   B   C
> Persian Gulf. No error
>   D   E
> The correct answer is (C).

1. Irregardless of the consequences,
     A   B
   the Light Brigade followed orders
                        C
   and charged into the fray.
       D
   No error
    E

2. Everybody in the room
   demonstrated his enthusiasm by
              A
   the loud welcome he gave the
                   B
   team which had just returned
        C   D
   after winning the pennant.

   No error
    E

3. The headmaster was angry when
                    A
   he was informed of John coming
                    B
   late to class and being
    C   D
   unprepared. No error
             E

4. Often considered a member of
        A
   the rat family, the water vole
   can be distinguished from the
               B
   common rat by the smallness of
   its ears and looking at the
              C
   bluntness of its face. No error
           D   E

5. Everybody in <u>the school</u>
                  A
    population <u>have been</u> guaranteed
               B
    an opportunity to get a

    <u>liberal education</u> and <u>to learn</u>
    C   D
    a trade. <u>No error</u>
             E

6. <u>Because</u> he had been asked to
    A
    speak to the class, he <u>tells</u> the
                           B
    students about his experiences <u>as</u>
                                    C
    a waiter in a <u>summer</u> hotel.
                   D
    <u>No error</u>
    E

7. Unless upper and lower

    <u>molar</u> patterns are examined and
    A
    <u>recorded</u>, the zoology student
    B
    <u>will not</u> be able to identify the
    C
    species <u>at</u> any degree of
             D
    accuracy. <u>No error</u>
              E

8. When Philip <u>was</u> in camp for
                A
    three days, he <u>became</u> homesick
                    B
    and tried to <u>run</u> home to
                  C
    <u>his parents</u> and friends. <u>No error</u>
    D   E

9. When the bell <u>rang</u> and the
                   A   B
    students marched <u>into</u> the
                      C
    auditorium for their morning

    meeting with the <u>principal.</u>
                      D
    <u>No error</u>
    E

10. I felt <u>then</u>, and <u>I feel now</u>, very
           A   B
    <u>badly</u> about my refusal
    C
    to participate in <u>the school</u>
                       D
    pageant. <u>No error</u>
             E

11. A variety of <u>exotic</u> tropical <u>fish</u>
                  A   B
    and birds as well as

    <u>more mundane</u> pets like dogs,
    C
    cats, and canaries <u>is</u> on sale at
                        D
    the Annual Animal Fair.

    <u>No error</u>
    E

12. Diet, shelter, and

    <u>being free</u> to breed <u>are factors</u>
    A   B
    <u>which</u> determine the <u>rapidity</u>
    C   D
    of rodent population growth.

    <u>No error</u>
    E

13. Although I <u>have rode</u> the
                A
    subways for many years, I

    <u>have not become adjusted</u> to the
    B
    <u>noise</u> and filth in the <u>trains.</u>
    C   D
    <u>No error</u>
    E

14. <u>If I would have known</u> the
    A
    consequences of <u>my</u> actions, I
                     B
    <u>would not have behaved the way</u>
    C
    <u>I did.</u> <u>No error</u>
    D   E

15. <u>Because</u> we knew him so
    A
    intimately <u>while</u> he was alive, we
               B
    are all the <u>more richer</u> and aware
                C
    of the <u>necessity</u> of continuing his
            D
    great work. <u>No error</u>
                 E

16. When the <u>news</u> about the release
                A
    of the hostages <u>was announced,</u>
                     B
    all of us felt <u>real</u> <u>good.</u> <u>No error</u>
                   C   D   E

17. If the sender of this letter
$\overline{A}$
was aware of the anger he had
$\overline{B}$
aroused, he might have been less
$\overline{C}$ $\overline{D}$
irritating. No error
$\overline{E}$

18. When I am offered a choice of
$\overline{A}$
meat or fish at a restaurant, I
$\overline{B}$
invariably choose the latter.
$\overline{C}$ $\overline{D}$
No error
$\overline{E}$

19. The President has designated
$\overline{A}$
Senator Frank as one of the
$\overline{B}$
Congressmen who is going to
$\overline{C}$
attend the funeral of Queen
$\overline{D}$
Dorothy of Ruritania. No error
$\overline{E}$

20. A sudden downpour drenched the
$\overline{A}$ $\overline{B}$
area where we had been laying
$\overline{C}$
and forced all the people at the
pool to leave their beach chairs
$\overline{D}$
and rush to their cabanas.

No error
$\overline{E}$

21. When the car was repaired at the
$\overline{A}$ $\overline{B}$
shop, either the muffler or the
$\overline{C}$
exhaust pipe were replaced.
$\overline{D}$
No error
$\overline{E}$

22. The average citizen today is
surprisingly knowledgeable about
$\overline{A}$
landmark court decisions
concerning such questions as
$\overline{B}$ $\overline{C}$
racial segregation, legislative
appointment, prayer in the
public schools, and the right of a
defendant to counsel in a
$\overline{D}$
criminal prosecution. No error
$\overline{E}$

23. The Commission hopes to reduce
$\overline{A}$
the high rate of inflation and to
$\overline{B}$
have less people unemployed in
$\overline{C}$
the near future. No error
$\overline{D}$ $\overline{E}$

24. The reason the three girls were
$\overline{A}$
late to the party was because
$\overline{B}$ $\overline{C}$
they took the wrong train at the
$\overline{D}$
station. No error
$\overline{E}$

25. Frank went to the steam room
$\overline{A}$
after he had swam twenty laps in
$\overline{B}$ $\overline{C}$
the school pool. No error
$\overline{D}$ $\overline{E}$

Directions: In each sentence below, some or all of the words are underlined. The portion underlined may be correct or it may contain an error in grammar, diction, style, or punctuation. The sentence is followed by five possible ways of writing the underlined portion. If you think the underlined portion is correct in the original sentence, you will choose (A) as your answer, because (A) repeats the underlined section. If you think the underlined portion is incorrect, you will select the group of words from choices (B), (C), (D) or (E) which best corrects the error you have found. Do not select a choice which changes the meaning of the original sentence.

Example: Although I calculate that he will be here any minute, I cannot wait much longer for him to arrive.

(A) Although I calculate that he will be here

(B) Although I reckon that he will be here

(C) Because I calculate that he will be here

(D) Although I am confident that he will be here

(E) Because I am confident that he will be here

The correct answer is (D).

---

26. Complaining that he couldn't hear hardly anything, he asked Dr. Brown, the otologist, whether he should get a hearing aid.

(A) Complaining that he couldn't hear hardly anything,

(B) Complaining that he couldn't hardly hear anything,

(C) He complained that he couldn't hardly hear anything,

(D) Complaining that he could hear hardly anything,

(E) Because he couldn't hear hardly anything,

27. Shakespeare wrote many plays, they are now being presented on public television.

(A) Shakespeare wrote many plays, they are now being presented on public television.

(B) Shakespeare wrote many plays, and they have been presented on public television.

(C) Shakespeare wrote many plays, which public television has now presented.

(D) The many plays of Shakespeare have now been presented on public television.

(E) Shakespeare wrote many plays; they are now being presented on public television.

28. Many alcoholics attempt to conceal their problem from their fellow workers, but invariably failing to keep their secret.

(A) but invariably failing to keep their secret

(B) but they invariably fail to keep their secret

(C) but fail, invariably, to keep their secret

(D) who invariably fail to keep their secret

(E) who they invariably fail to keep their secret from

29. Upon considering the facts of the case, the solution was obvious; consequently, Holmes sent for the police.

(A) Upon considering

(B) When considering

(C) Considering

(D) On consideration of

(E) When he considered

30. Familiar with the terrain from previous visits, <u>the explorer's search for the abandoned mine site was a success</u>.

    (A) the explorer's search for the abandoned mine site was a success

    (B) the success of the explorer's search for the abandoned mine site was assured

    (C) the explorer succeeded in finding the abandoned mine site

    (D) the search by the explorer for the abandoned mine was successful

    (E) the explorer in his search for the abandoned mine site was a success

31. Economic conditions demand <u>not only cutting wages and prices but also to reduce</u> inflation-raised tax rates.

    (A) not only cutting wages and prices but also to reduce

    (B) we not only cut wages and prices but also reduce

    (C) to not only cut wages and prices but also to reduce

    (D) not only to cut wages and prices but also to reduce

    (E) not only a cut in wages and prices but also to reduce

32. He interviewed several candidates <u>who he thought</u> had the experience and qualifications he required.

    (A) who he thought

    (B) whom he thought

    (C) of whom he thought

    (D) he thought who

    (E) which he thought

33. A person's true character, it seems, is revealed <u>in a situation which is similar to this</u>.

    (A) in a situation which is similar to this

    (B) in a situation like this is

    (C) in a situation such as this

    (D) in such a situation like this is

    (E) from a situation such as this

34. It is typical of military service for a skilled technician to be inducted and <u>then you spend your whole tour of duty</u> peeling potatoes and cleaning latrines.

    (A) then you spend your whole tour of duty

    (B) to spend your whole tour of duty

    (C) then they spend their whole tour of duty

    (D) to spend their whole tour of duty

    (E) then spend his whole tour of duty

35. <u>Being that he is that kind of a boy</u>, he should not be blamed for his mistakes.

    (A) Being that he is that kind of a boy,

    (B) Being that he is that kind of boy,

    (C) Since he is that kind of boy,

    (D) Since he is that sort of a boy,

    (E) Because he is that sort of a boy,

36. At an early stage in his travels, <u>Henry James writing</u> from abroad described the subtle differences distinguishing Americans from Europeans.

   (A) At an early stage in his travels, Henry James writing

   (B) At an early stage in his travels, Henry James wrote

   (C) At an early stage in his travels, Henry James while writing

   (D) At an early stage in his travels, Henry James was writing

   (E) Henry James, whose writing at an early stage in his travels

37. <u>Fame as well as fortune were his goals in life.</u>

   (A) Fame as well as fortune were his goals in life.

   (B) Fame as well as fortune was his goals in life.

   (C) Fame as well as fortune were his goal in life.

   (D) Fame and fortune were his goals in life.

   (E) Fame also fortune were his goals in life.

38. For recreation I like to watch <u>these kind of</u> programs in the evening.

   (A) these kind of

   (B) these sort of

   (C) these kinds of

   (D) them kinds of

   (E) this kinds of

39. Whatever the surface indications of the moment may be, modern men are basically <u>less tolerant of despots then the men of old.</u>

   (A) less tolerant of despots then the men of old

   (B) less tolerant of despots than older men

   (C) less tolerant of despots than of men of old ·

   (D) more intolerant of despots then in former years

   (E) less tolerant of despots than the men of old

40. During the morning hours, Frances attended school, but in the afternoon, <u>watching soap operas occupied her time.</u>

   (A) watching soap operas occupied her time

   (B) she spent her time in the watching of soap operas

   (C) her time was spent watching soap operas

   (D) she watched soap operas

   (E) soap opera watching took up her time

Directions: In each of the sentences below, there are four underlined words or phrases. If you think there is an error in usage, grammar, diction, or punctuation in any of the underlined parts, write the letter indicated on your answer paper. If there is no error in any of the underlined parts, mark (E) on your answer paper.

Example: The aircraft carrier with all her accompanying ships are going to sail to the
$\quad\quad\quad\quad\quad\quad$ A $\quad\quad\quad\quad\quad\quad\quad\quad$ B $\quad\quad\quad\quad$ C

Persian Gulf. No error
$\quad$ D $\quad\quad$ E

The correct answer is (C).

---

41. I have came to the conclusion
$\quad\quad$ A $\quad\quad\quad\quad$ B
that everyone in this room

has conspired to keep the bad
$\quad\quad$ C
news from me. No error
$\quad\quad$ D $\quad\quad$ E

42. I must admit that your excuse for
$\quad$ A
your failure to complete the
$\quad$ B
assignment is the most unique
$\quad\quad\quad\quad\quad\quad$ C
one I have ever heard. No error
$\quad\quad\quad\quad$ D $\quad\quad\quad$ E

43. Although most Californians
$\quad\quad$ A
believe that they are due to have
$\quad\quad\quad\quad\quad\quad$ B
a serious earthquake in the near
$\quad\quad\quad\quad\quad\quad\quad\quad$ C
future, they are not frightened by
$\quad\quad\quad$ D
that possibility. No error
$\quad\quad\quad\quad$ E

44. The jury, in their infinite wisdom,
$\quad\quad\quad\quad\quad$ A
has reached a decision and
$\quad$ B $\quad\quad\quad$ C
will now report to the judge.
$\quad\quad$ D
No error
$\quad$ E

45. Burglary is where a person
$\quad\quad\quad$ A
breaks and enters a dwelling
$\quad\quad\quad$ B
at night with the intention
$\quad$ C
of committing a felony. No error
$\quad$ D $\quad\quad\quad\quad$ E

46. Examining the test papers
$\quad\quad$ A
carefully, evidences of cheating
$\quad\quad$ B $\quad\quad\quad\quad\quad$ C
were discovered, which were
$\quad\quad\quad\quad$ D
brought to the attention of the

dean. No error
$\quad$ E

47. Give the money you collect to
$\quad\quad\quad\quad\quad\quad$ A
either John or I; both of us are
$\quad$ B $\quad\quad\quad$ C $\quad\quad\quad\quad$ D
the treasurers of the club.

No error
$\quad$ E

48. The owners of the restaurant

planned to have opened an
$\quad\quad\quad\quad\quad\quad$ A
addition to the dining room
$\quad\quad\quad$ B $\quad\quad\quad$ C
which could be used for private
$\quad\quad\quad\quad$ D
parties, weddings, and meetings.

No error
$\quad$ E

49. I intend to call this matter to the
$\quad\quad\quad\quad$ A
attention of whomever is
$\quad\quad$ B $\quad\quad$ C
in charge of the service
$\quad\quad\quad\quad$ D
station. No error
$\quad\quad$ E

50. I could scarcely recognize him
$\quad\quad\quad\quad$ A
when he came out of the
$\quad\quad\quad$ B
hospital; he was so haggard and
$\quad\quad\quad\quad\quad\quad$ C
emaciated. No error
$\quad$ D $\quad\quad$ E

STOP
END OF TYPICAL TEST A

Answer Key—Typical Test A

1. A	11. D	21. D	31. B	41. A
2. E	12. A	22. E	32. A	42. C
3. B	13. A	23. C	33. C	43. E
4. C	14. A	24. C	34. E	44. B
5. B	15. C	25. C	35. C	45. A
6. B	16. D	26. D	36. A	46. A
7. D	17. B	27. E	37. D	47. C
8. A	18. E	28. B	38. C	48. A
9. A	19. C	29. E	39. E	49. C
10. C	20. C	30. C	40. D	50. E

Item Classification Chart—Typical Test A

Error	Question	See Page
Fragment	9	47, 75
Run-on	27	75
Subject-verb Agreement	5, 11, 19, 21, 37, 44, 45	76
Pronoun-Antecedent Agreement	34	76
Pronoun Reference		56
Case	3, 47, 49	27, 54, 76
Unclear Placement of Modifier		
Dangling Modifier	29, 30, 46	59, 77
Parallel Structure	4, 12, 28, 31, 40	60, 77
Sequence of Tenses	6, 8, 48	57
Mood	14, 17	58
Verb Conjugation	13, 25, 41	30
Transitive — Intransitive verbs	20	39
Adjective Comparison	15	
Adjective-Adverb Confusion	10, 16	77
Double Negative	26	
Diction	1, 23, 24, 33, 35, 38, 39, 42	77
Idiomatic Expression	7	65
No Error in Question	2, 18, 22, 32, 36, 43, 50	

How Well Did You Do on Typical Test A?

1. Find your raw score.

    a. Count the number of correct answers.

    b. Count the number of incorrect answers. (Do not count blanks as incorrect answers.)

    c. Use this formula to find your raw score:

    Raw Score = Number Correct − ¼ Number Incorrect

    Example: A student answers 41 questions correctly. He answers seven incorrectly and leaves two questions unanswered. His raw score is 41 − 1.75 (one-fourth of 7) which equals 39.25.

2. Evaluate your raw score.

Raw Score	Evaluation
45 to 50	Superior
39 to 44	Above average
33 to 38	Average
15 to 32	May need remedial work in college
Below 15	Definitely needs remedial work

How Can You Profit from This Test?

1. Look at the explanation of answers which follows this page. Notice the areas where you made your errors.

2. Chapters 3–5 of this book contain a review of the important elements of grammar, diction, style, and punctuation covered in this test. Study the sections which discuss the areas where you made your errors. If you scored low on this test, you should review all three chapters.

3. Go on to Typical Test B.

Answers Explained—Typical Test A

1. **A**   *Irregardless* is nonstandard English. Change to *Regardless*.
2. **E**   Choices (A), (B), (C), and (D) are correct.
3. **B**   Error in the case of *John*. A noun or pronoun preceding a gerund (*coming*) should be in the possessive case. Change to *John's*.
4. **C**   The lack of parallel structure can be corrected by deleting the phrase *looking at*.
5. **B**   Error in agreement between subject and verb. The singular pronoun *everybody* should be followed by the singular verb *has been*.

6. **B**   Sequence of tenses is violated in this sentence. The verb in the subordinate clause (*had been asked*) is in the past perfect tense. The present tense in the principal clause is inaccurate. Change *tells* to *told*.

7. **D**   The expression *at any degree of accuracy* is idiomatically incorrect. Change *at* to *with*.

8. **A**   Error in tense. The past perfect tense is needed to indicate that one event occurred before another event. Change *was* to *had been*.

9. **A**   This group of words, introduced by the conjunction *when*, is a subordinate clause and, therefore, a sentence fragment. The elimination of *when* makes the group of words a good sentence.

10. **C**   The verb *feel* is a copulative verb and should be followed by a predicate adjective rather than an adverb. Change *badly* to *bad*.

11. **D**   Error in agreement. The expression *a variety* is plural and should be followed by the plural verb *are*.

12. **A**   Parallel structure would be maintained by changing the phrase *being free to breed* to *freedom to breed*.

13. **A**   Error in the use of the past participle of *ride*. Change *have rode* to *have ridden*.

14. **A**   Error in the formation of the subjunctive mood. Change *would have known* to *had known*.

15. **C**   The comparative form of the adjective *rich* is *richer*.

16. **D**   To modify an adjective, an adverb must be used. Change *real* to *really*.

17. **B**   A verb in the subjunctive mood is required in the *if* clause, because it states a condition contrary to fact. (The sender was *not* aware of the anger he had aroused.) Change *was aware* to *were aware*.

18. **E**   Choices (A), (B), (C), and (D) are all correct.

19. **C**   Error in agreement between subject and verb. The subject of the verb *is going* is the pronoun *who*. The antecedent of *who* is *Congressmen* (plural). Since *who* in this sentence is plural, it should be followed by a plural verb. Change *is going* to *are going*.

20. **C**   The verb in the clause *where we had been laying* has no object and, therefore, is intransitive. *Laying* is the present participle of the transitive verb *to lay*; this sentence calls for the intransitive verb *lie* instead. Change *had been laying* to *had been lying*.

21. **D**   Error in agreement. In an *either . . . or* construction, the verb agrees in number with the noun or pronoun that follows *or*. Change *were repaired* to *was repaired*.

22. **E**   Choices (A), (B), (C), and (D) are all correct.

23. **C**   Error in diction. *Fewer* should be used instead of *less* in this sentence, since unemployed people may be counted.

24. **C**   The expression *the reason was* should be followed by a noun clause instead of an adverbial clause. Change *because* to *that*.

25. **C**   Improper conjugation of the verb *to swim*. The past perfect tense of *swim* is *had swum*.

26. **D**   Choice (D) corrects the double negative found in the other four choices. Note that, grammatically, *hardly* is considered a negative word. Choice (C), in addition, creates a run-on sentence.

27. **E**   Choice (A) is a run-on sentence. Choices (B), (C), and (D) change the meaning of the original sentence. They indicate that the plays have already been presented; the original sentence states that these plays are being presented at the present time. Choice (E) corrects the run-on without altering the meaning of the sentence.

28. **B**   In choice (A), the conjunction *but* should be followed by a clause to parallel the clause in the first half of the sentence. Choice (B) provides such a clause. The awkward placement of the word *invariably* in choice (C) makes the sentence very unclear. The use of *who* in choices (D) and (E) leads to ambiguity because it may be taken to refer to *workers*.

29. **E** Choices (A), (B), and (C) are incorrect because of the dangling participle *considering*. Choice (D) changes the meaning of the sentence.

30. **C** In choices (A), (B), and (D), the modifier *familiar* is dangling. The wording in choice (E) suggests that the explorer was a success, whereas the original sentence states that the search was a success—a somewhat different meaning. Choice (C) corrects the error and retains the original meaning of the sentence.

31. **B** Choices (A), (C), and (E) do not maintain parallel structure. Choice (B) corrects this weakness. The infinitive *to cut* cannot be an object of *demand*, as in choice (D); a noun clause like the one in choice (B) corrects this error.

32. **A** Choice (A) is correct because the subject of the verb *had* must be *who* and not *whom*. *Which* in choice (E) should not be used to refer to a person.

33. **C** In choices (B) and (D), the preposition *like* is used incorrectly as a conjunction. The use of *from* in choice (E) is idiomatically incorrect. Choice (A) creates an awkward and needlessly wordy sentence.

34. **E** The pronouns *you* and *your* in the second clause of the sentence refer to *technician*, which is a third person singular noun. The pronoun, therefore, should be the third person singular *his*.

35. **C** There are two errors in the underlined portion of this sentence: the expression *being that* is nonstandard, and the phrase *kind of* or *sort of* should not be followed by *a* or *an*.

36. **A** As used in choice (A), *writing* is a participle modifying *James*. In choices (B), (C), and (D), the use of a verb (*wrote, was written,* or *was writing*) without the use of a conjunction to connect with *described* creates a grammatically incorrect sentence. The change in choice (E) results in a sentence fragment.

37. **D** In the original sentence, the subject is *fame*, a singular noun. Therefore, the verb should also be singular. This eliminates choices (A) and (C). In choice (B), *goals* should be *goal*. The word *also* in choice (E) should not be used as a conjunction.

38. **C** The plural expressions *kinds of* and *sorts of* should be modified by *these* and *those*.

39. **E** *Then* is incorrectly used in this sentence. The correct word is *than*. Choices (B) and (C) change the meaning of the sentence.

40. **D** Choice (D) correctly parallels the structure of the first half of the sentence.

41. **A** The past participle of *come* is *come*. Therefore, the present perfect tense is *have come*.

42. **C** *Unique* should not be modified by a qualifying word like *most*. Change *unique* to *unusual*.

43. **E** The sentence is correct.

44. **B** *Jury*, a collective noun, may be considered either singular or plural. The pronoun *their* indicates that, in this sentence, the antecedent *jury* is plural; however, the verb *has reached* is singular. Since the pronoun *their* is not underlined, we cannot change it and must assume that it is correct. Therefore, the verb must agree with a plural subject. *Has reached* should be changed to *have reached*.

45. **A** The copulative verb *to be* should not be followed by a clause introduced by *where*. Choice (A) should be changed to a phrase like *a crime in which*.

46. **A** *Examining* is a dangling participle. The sentence should be rewritten to read something like: *When the proctors examined the test papers carefully, . . .*

47. **C** The pronoun *I* is one of the two objects of the preposition *to*. Therefore, it should be in the objective case. Change *I* to *me*.

48. **A** The tense of the infinitive is incorrect. Change *to have opened* to *to open*.

49. **C** The subject of the verb *is* should be the nominative case pronoun *whoever*.

50. **E** The sentence is correct.

answer sheet–typical test b

To the student:

Take the following test under examination conditions.

Have on hand a supply of #2 pencils and a good eraser.

Limit yourself to thirty minutes.

Because you will be penalized for wrong answers, do not guess wildly. However, if you can eliminate some of the choices, you can improve your score by guessing.

The answer grid below is provided for your convenience. Fill in the oval which contains the letter of your choice. You may remove this page from the book for ease in marking your answers.

1. Ⓐ Ⓑ Ⓒ Ⓓ Ⓔ   27. Ⓐ Ⓑ Ⓒ Ⓓ Ⓔ   14. Ⓐ Ⓑ Ⓒ Ⓓ Ⓔ   40. Ⓐ Ⓑ Ⓒ Ⓓ Ⓔ
2. Ⓐ Ⓑ Ⓒ Ⓓ Ⓔ   28. Ⓐ Ⓑ Ⓒ Ⓓ Ⓔ   15. Ⓐ Ⓑ Ⓒ Ⓓ Ⓔ   41. Ⓐ Ⓑ Ⓒ Ⓓ Ⓔ
3. Ⓐ Ⓑ Ⓒ Ⓓ Ⓔ   29. Ⓐ Ⓑ Ⓒ Ⓓ Ⓔ   16. Ⓐ Ⓑ Ⓒ Ⓓ Ⓔ   42. Ⓐ Ⓑ Ⓒ Ⓓ Ⓔ
4. Ⓐ Ⓑ Ⓒ Ⓓ Ⓔ   30. Ⓐ Ⓑ Ⓒ Ⓓ Ⓔ   17. Ⓐ Ⓑ Ⓒ Ⓓ Ⓔ   43. Ⓐ Ⓑ Ⓒ Ⓓ Ⓔ
5. Ⓐ Ⓑ Ⓒ Ⓓ Ⓔ   31. Ⓐ Ⓑ Ⓒ Ⓓ Ⓔ   18. Ⓐ Ⓑ Ⓒ Ⓓ Ⓔ   44. Ⓐ Ⓑ Ⓒ Ⓓ Ⓔ
6. Ⓐ Ⓑ Ⓒ Ⓓ Ⓔ   32. Ⓐ Ⓑ Ⓒ Ⓓ Ⓔ   19. Ⓐ Ⓑ Ⓒ Ⓓ Ⓔ   45. Ⓐ Ⓑ Ⓒ Ⓓ Ⓔ
7. Ⓐ Ⓑ Ⓒ Ⓓ Ⓔ   33. Ⓐ Ⓑ Ⓒ Ⓓ Ⓔ   20. Ⓐ Ⓑ Ⓒ Ⓓ Ⓔ   46. Ⓐ Ⓑ Ⓒ Ⓓ Ⓔ
8. Ⓐ Ⓑ Ⓒ Ⓓ Ⓔ   34. Ⓐ Ⓑ Ⓒ Ⓓ Ⓔ   21. Ⓐ Ⓑ Ⓒ Ⓓ Ⓔ   47. Ⓐ Ⓑ Ⓒ Ⓓ Ⓔ
9. Ⓐ Ⓑ Ⓒ Ⓓ Ⓔ   35. Ⓐ Ⓑ Ⓒ Ⓓ Ⓔ   22. Ⓐ Ⓑ Ⓒ Ⓓ Ⓔ   48. Ⓐ Ⓑ Ⓒ Ⓓ Ⓔ
10. Ⓐ Ⓑ Ⓒ Ⓓ Ⓔ   36. Ⓐ Ⓑ Ⓒ Ⓓ Ⓔ   23. Ⓐ Ⓑ Ⓒ Ⓓ Ⓔ   49. Ⓐ Ⓑ Ⓒ Ⓓ Ⓔ
11. Ⓐ Ⓑ Ⓒ Ⓓ Ⓔ   37. Ⓐ Ⓑ Ⓒ Ⓓ Ⓔ   24. Ⓐ Ⓑ Ⓒ Ⓓ Ⓔ   50. Ⓐ Ⓑ Ⓒ Ⓓ Ⓔ
12. Ⓐ Ⓑ Ⓒ Ⓓ Ⓔ   38. Ⓐ Ⓑ Ⓒ Ⓓ Ⓔ   25. Ⓐ Ⓑ Ⓒ Ⓓ Ⓔ
13. Ⓐ Ⓑ Ⓒ Ⓓ Ⓔ   39. Ⓐ Ⓑ Ⓒ Ⓓ Ⓔ   26. Ⓐ Ⓑ Ⓒ Ⓓ Ⓔ

chapter 8

typical test b

Time: 30 minutes   50 questions

Directions: In each of the sentences below, there are four underlined words or phrases. If you think there is an error in usage, grammar, diction, or punctuation in one of the underlined parts, write the letter indicated on your answer paper. If there is no error in any of the underlined parts, mark (E) on your answer paper.

Example: The aircraft carrier with all her accompanying ships are going to sail to the
              A   B   C

Persian Gulf. No error
     D   E
The correct answer is (C).

---

1. I agree that I have spoke to you
        A   B
    many times about the condition
                  C
    of your room, but I do not call
                     D
    that "nagging." No error
                     E

2. If I was going to be "catty," I
        A
    could tell you many things about
              B
    our friend which would surprise
                C   D
    and shock you. No error
                    E

3. Mr. Adams said that he wants
              A   B
    you and I to go to the airport
            C
    and drive Mrs. Adams home
                            D
    when her plane arrives. No error
                             E

4. On the basis of his test scores,
            A
    John seems to be as intelligent, if
                        B
    not more intelligent than any
            C
    other student in his grade.
            D
    No error
    E

5. There <u>appears</u> to <u>be many</u>
       A   B
   similarities <u>between</u> your report
               C
   and the one <u>handed in</u> by Miss
                 D
   Jones. <u>No error</u>
          E

6. Fred Brown <u>has lived</u>
             A
   <u>in this house</u> <u>for ten years</u>
        B   C
   before he <u>went to work</u> for the
               D
   Bethlehem Steel Corporation.

   <u>No error</u>
     E

7. <u>Believing</u> that his friends
     A
   <u>had remained</u> loyal to him when
        B
   many people <u>were abandoning</u>
               C
   the movement <u>which</u> had been
             D
   their only hope. <u>No error</u>
             E

8. <u>Gazing</u> through my
     A
   binoculars, the bird <u>was</u> one I
            B
   <u>had never seen</u> in this <u>area of</u>
       C   D
   the country. <u>No error</u>
           E

9. As I sat watching the sun <u>slowly</u>
    A   B
   sink toward the rim of the

   mountain range <u>beyond</u> the Rift
              C
   Valley, I <u>became</u> aware of a
           D
   strange silence. <u>No error</u>
            E

10. Neither Frank <u>or</u> Henry <u>returned</u>
              A   B
    the overdue books to the library

    when asked by the <u>authorities</u> to
            C   D
    do so. <u>No error</u>
         E

11. This is a <u>shelter</u> <u>where</u> actors
            A   B
    and dancers <u>which</u> are "at
             C

liberty" can get food and clothing

while they look for jobs. <u>No error</u>
  D   E

12. To <u>watch</u> a football game
        A
    <u>intelligently</u>, a knowledge
       B
    <u>of the rules</u> and of the function
        C
    of <u>each</u> player is invaluable.
        D
    <u>No error</u>
      E

13. I <u>do not understand</u> <u>what</u> you
          A   B
    are trying to <u>infer</u> by the
             C
    statement you have <u>just</u> issued to
                 D
    the press. <u>No error</u>
          E

14. <u>Hoping</u> that he <u>would receive</u>
      A   B
    bipartisan support in Congress,

    the President submitted a

    legislative program <u>which</u> he
               C
    believed would alleviate the

    economic <u>ills</u> of the country.
            D
    <u>No error</u>
      E

15. She <u>reached for</u> the telephone
        A
    <u>to call</u> the police when she heard
      B
    the noise of the <u>burglar</u> breaking
              C
    <u>into</u> the house. <u>No error</u>
      D   E

16. With the <u>addition</u> of the new
           A
    equipment, our word processor

    is <u>as good</u>, if not <u>better than</u> the
       B   C
    one we <u>used</u> to have. <u>No error</u>
          D   E

17. Sam and <u>him</u>, after days of futile
          A
    searching, <u>abandoned</u> <u>their plans</u>
          B   C
    to find the sunken ship and

    to salvage its contents. <u>No error</u>
      D   E

18. When we <u>misbehaved</u>, the
      A
    teacher said <u>that</u> he <u>wasn't going</u>
      B   C
    to warn us but once before
    <u>reporting</u> us to the dean. <u>No error</u>
      D   E

19. The oarsman <u>tried</u> to keep the
      A
    raft <u>away from</u> the treacherous
      B
    rocks, a <u>huge</u> wave almost
      C
    <u>swamped</u> the tiny craft. <u>No error</u>
      D   E

20. <u>In my history class</u> I learned
      A
    <u>why</u> the American colonies
      B
    <u>opposed</u> the British, how they
      C
    organized the militia, and the
    <u>work of the Continental Congress.</u>
      D
    <u>No error</u>
      E

21. The audience <u>became</u> restless
      A
    and <u>noisy</u> when the curtain did
      B
    not <u>raise</u> at the <u>scheduled</u> time.
      C   D
    <u>No error</u>
      E

22. Dr. Brown <u>advised</u> Mr. Bayan to
      A
    move to Arizona because the
    <u>healthier</u> climate in <u>that</u> area
      B   C
    would be helpful in <u>controlling</u>
      D
    his asthmatic condition. <u>No error</u>
      E

23. He <u>was warned</u> that if he
      A
    <u>did not have</u> the operation
      B
    <u>within a year</u> he <u>would be</u> blind.
      C   D
    <u>No error</u>
      E

24. The fire officials <u>attributed</u> the
      A
    high casualty rate to the fact that
    not one of the <u>more than</u> two
      B
    thousand rooms in the hotel
    <u>were equipped</u> with sprinklers <u>or</u>
      C   D
    smoke detectors. <u>No error</u>
      E

25. Although the Raiders <u>were</u> the
      A   B
    underdogs, they took an early
    lead and <u>managed</u> to hold on to
      C
    <u>it</u> until the game ended.
      D
    <u>No error</u>
      E

Directions: In each sentence below, some or all of the words are underlined. The portion underlined may be correct or it may contain an error in grammar, diction, style, or punctuation. The sentence is followed by five possible ways of writing the underlined portion. If you think the underlined portion is correct in the original sentence, you will choose (A) as your answer, because (A) repeats the underlined section. If you think the underlined portion is incorrect, you will select the group of words from choices (B), (C), (D) or (E) which best corrects the error you have found. Do not select a choice which changes the meaning of the original sentence.

Example: Although I calculate that he will be here any minute, I cannot wait much longer for him to arrive.

   (A)   Although I calculate that he will be here

   (B)   Although I reckon that he will be here

   (C)   Because I calculate that he will be here

   (D)   Although I am confident that he will be here

   (E)   Because I am confident that he will be here

The correct answer is (D).

---

26. By the time we arrive in Italy, we have traveled through four countries.

   (A)   we have traveled through four countries

   (B)   we had traveled through four countries

   (C)   we will have traveled through four countries

   (D)   four countries will have been traveled through

   (E)   we through four countries shall have traveled

27. To say "My lunch was satisfactory" is complimentary, to say "My lunch is adequate" is not.

   (A)   complimentary, to say

   (B)   complementary; to say

   (C)   complementary, however, to say

   (D)   complimentary, but to say

   (E)   complementary to saying

28. When one debates the merits of the proposed reduction in our tax base, you should take into consideration the effect it will have on the schools and the other public services.

   (A)   you should take into consideration the effect

   (B)   you should consider the effect

   (C)   he should consider the affect

   (D)   he takes into consideration the affect

   (E)   he should take into consideration the effect

29. We were afraid of the teacher's wrath, due to his statement that he would penalize anyone who failed to hand in his term paper on time.

    (A)   wrath, due to his statement that

    (B)   wrath due to his statement that

    (C)   wrath, inasmuch as his statement that

    (D)   wrath because of his statement that

    (E)   wrath and his statement that

30. Although the doctors had put the patient through a series of tests, including X-rays and cystoscopy, they have found no explanation of her mysterious ailment.

    (A)   they have found no explanation of her mysterious ailment

    (B)   no explanation of her mysterious ailment has been found

    (C)   no explanation was found of her mysterious ailment

    (D)   they did not explain her mysterious ailment

    (E)   they found no explanation of her mysterious ailment

31. Originally referring to an excess of patriotic fervor, the term "chauvinism" has come to signify devotion to the theory of masculine superiority.

    (A)   Originally referring to an excess of patriotic fervor,

    (B)   In its original reference to an excess of patriotic fervor,

    (C)   Originally it referred to an excess of patriotic fervor,

    (D)   Originally it was referring to excessive patriotic fervor,

    (E)   An excess of patriotic fervor being originally referred to,

32. Exercise offers both physical and emotional benefits: a sense of control over one's body, a feeling of accomplishment, and it is a release of pent-up frustrations.

    (A)   and it is a release of pent-up frustrations

    (B)   and it releases pent-up frustrations

    (C)   by releasing pent-up frustrations

    (D)   and a release of pent-up frustrations

    (E)   and a release from pent-up frustrations

33. If the Confederate Army would have carried the day at Gettysburg, the history of America during the past century would have been profoundly altered.

    (A)   If the Confederate Army would have carried the day at Gettysburg,

    (B)   Had the Confederate Army carried the day at Gettysburg,

    (C)   The Confederate Army having carried the day at Gettysburg,

    (D)   If the Confederate Army would have won at Gettysburg,

    (E)   If the Battle of Gettysburg would have been won by the Confederate Army,

34. I have discovered that the subways in New York are as clean as any other city I have visited.

    (A)   as clean as any other city I have visited

    (B)   as clean as those in any other city I have visited

    (C)   as clean as those in any city I visited

    (D)   cleaner than any city I visited

    (E)   cleaner than any city I have visited

35. Inflation in the United States <u>has not and, we hope, never will reach</u> a rate of 20 per cent a year.

    (A) has not and, we hope, never will reach
    (B) has not reached and, we hope, never will
    (C) has not and hopefully never will reach
    (D) has not reached and, we hope, never will reach
    (E) has not reached and hopefully never will

36. <u>Arriving at the scene of the accident, the victims of the crash were treated by the paramedics.</u>

    (A) Arriving at the scene of the accident, the victims of the crash were treated by the paramedics.
    (B) At the scene of the accident, the paramedics treated the victims of the crash.
    (C) As soon as they had arrived at the scene of the accident, the paramedics treated the crash victims.
    (D) Arriving at the scene of the accident, the paramedics will treat the victims of the crash.
    (E) Arriving at the scene of the accident, the paramedics treated the victims of the crash.

37. <u>Since all the tickets to the show had been sold</u>, we went to a concert at Carnegie Hall.

    (A) Since all the tickets to the show had been sold
    (B) Being that all the tickets to the show had been sold
    (C) All the tickets to the show having been sold
    (D) Because they sold all the tickets to the show
    (E) Being that all the tickets to the show were sold

38. Although I understand why airlines have to serve frozen foods to their passengers, I do not understand why I was served <u>a meal by a flight attendant that had been only partially defrosted.</u>

    (A) a meal by a flight attendant that had been only partially defrosted
    (B) an only partially defrosted meal by a flight attendant
    (C) a meal that only had been partially defrosted by a flight attendant
    (D) by a flight attendant a meal that had only been partially defrosted
    (E) by a flight attendant of a partially defrosted meal

39. <u>If anyone asks for an application, send them</u> to room 1134 to see the personnel director.

    (A) If anyone asks for an application, send them
    (B) Send anyone who asks for an application
    (C) When anyone asks for an application, send them
    (D) If anyone asks for an application, they should be sent
    (E) As soon as anyone asks for an application, send them

40. I do not like these kind of mystery stories; I prefer stories with more action.

  (A) these kind of mystery stories;
  (B) these kind of mystery stories,
  (C) this kind of mystery stories,
  (D) these kinds of mystery stories;
  (E) these sorts of mystery stories,

Directions: In each of the sentences below, there are four underlined words or phrases. If you think there is an error in usage, grammar, diction, or punctuation in any of the underlined parts, write the letter indicated on your answer paper. If there is no error in any of the underlined parts, mark (E) on your answer paper.

> **Example:** The aircraft carrier with all her accompanying ships are going to sail to the
>   A   B   C
> Persian Gulf. No error
>   D   E
> The correct answer is (C).

41. The young orator spoke
           A   B
intelligently about her subject
              C
and with clarity and skill.
           D
No error
  E

42. In this restaurant, the variety of
    A
items offered as main courses are
       B   C
surprisingly limited. No error
      D   E

43. The price you are asking for
             A
these articles of furniture are
  B   C
ridiculous; I can buy them
elsewhere for half the amount.
    D
No error
  E

44. Given my choice of money as a
       A   B
reward or recognition of the
            C
value of my services, at this time
I would select the latter. No error
             D   E

45. In this battle for survival, we
       A
must act altogether as a single
         B   C
force or we will go down to
defeat one by one. No error
        D   E

46. The United States Military
Academy at West Point is one
             A
of the schools which
    B
has been established to train
       C
the men and women
who will become the officers in
         D
our armed forces. No error
         E

47. If you <u>would have been</u> with us
                  A
at the party <u>last</u> night, you
                  B
<u>would have met</u> <u>some</u>
         C   D
very interesting people. <u>No error</u>
                              E

48. When the <u>times</u> for the race
                    A
<u>were announced</u>, we learned that
         B
John <u>had finished the course</u>
                  C
faster than <u>me</u>. <u>No error</u>
                  D   E

49. Mrs. Rangel stated that after her
retirement she <u>intended</u> to travel,
                        A
to read the books
<u>which she had neglected</u>
              B
<u>because of</u> the pressure of
         C
business, and <u>to watch</u>
                        D
the progress of her grand-
children. <u>No error</u>
                  E

50. For the <u>next</u> two weeks, I want
                    A
the class <u>monitor</u> to be <u>he</u>
                  B   C
<u>who sits</u> in the last seat in the
         D
first row. <u>No error</u>
                  E

STOP
END OF TYPICAL TEST B

Answer Key—Typical Test B

1. **B**	11. **C**	21. **C**	31. **A**	41. **D**
2. **A**	12. **E**	22. **B**	32. **D**	42. **C**
3. **C**	13. **C**	23. **C**	33. **B**	43. **C**
4. **B**	14. **E**	24. **C**	34. **B**	44. **E**
5. **B**	15. **C**	25. **E**	35. **D**	45. **B**
6. **A**	16. **B**	26. **C**	36. **E**	46. **C**
7. **A**	17. **A**	27. **D**	37. **A**	47. **A**
8. **A**	18. **C**	28. **E**	38. **B**	48. **D**
9. **E**	19. **C**	29. **D**	39. **B**	49. **E**
10. **A**	20. **D**	30. **E**	40. **D**	50. **C**

Item Classification Chart—Typical Test B

Error	Question	See Page
Fragment	7	47, 75
Run-on	19, 27	75
Subject-verb Agreement	5, 24, 39, 42, 43, 46	76
Pronoun-Antecedent Agreement		76
Pronoun Reference	11, 28	56
Case	3, 15, 17, 48, 50	27, 54, 76
Unclear Placement of Modifier	23, 38	
Dangling Modifier	8, 36	59, 77
Parallel Structure	20, 32, 34, 41	60, 77
Sequence of Tenses	6, 26, 30	57
Mood	2, 33, 47	58
Verb Conjugation	1	30
Transitive — Intransitive Verbs	21	39
Adjective Comparison	4, 16	
Adjective-Adverb Confusion		77
Double Negative	18	
Diction	10, 13, 22, 29, 35, 40, 45	77
Idiomatic Expression		65
No Error in Question	9, 12, 14, 25, 31, 37, 44, 49	

How Well Did You Do on Typical Test B?

1. Find your raw score.

    a. Count the number of correct answers.

    b. Count the number of incorrect answers. (Do not count blanks as incorrect answers.)

    c. Use this formula to find your raw score:

    Raw Score = Number Correct − ¼ Number Incorrect

    Example: A student answers 41 questions correctly. He answers seven incorrectly and leaves two questions unanswered. His raw score is 41 − 1.75 (one-fourth of 7) which equals 39.25.

2. Evaluate your raw score.

Raw Score	Evaluation
45 to 50	Superior
39 to 44	Above average
33 to 38	Average
15 to 32	May need remedial work in college
Below 15	Definitely needs remedial work

How Can You Profit from This Test?

1. Look at the explanation of answers which follows this page. Notice the areas where you made your errors.

2. Chapters 3–5 of this book contain a review of the important elements of grammar, diction, style, and punctuation covered in this test. Study the sections which discuss the areas where you made your errors. If you scored low on this test, you should review all three chapters.

3. Go on to Typical Test C.

Answers Explained—Typical Test B

1. **B** Wrong form of the past participle of *speak*. The past participle of *speak* is *spoken*. Change *have spoke* to *have spoken*.

2. **A** The subjunctive mood is required when a condition contrary to fact is being described. In this sentence, the first clause describes such a condition: I am *not*, in fact, going to be "catty." Therefore, change *was going* to *were going*.

3. **B** Error in the case of the pronoun. Change *I* to *me*, because it is the subject of the infinitive *to go*.

4. **B** The comparison *as intelligent* is incomplete. The complete phrase should read *as intelligent as*.

5. **B** Lack of agreement between subject and verb. The plural subject, *similarities*, should go with a plural verb. Change *appears* to *appear*.

6. **A** Error in tense. The present perfect tense *has lived* is incorrect in this sentence because the action has been completed. The past perfect tense (*had lived*) should be used.

7. **A** This is a sentence fragment. There is no independent clause. Change *Believing* to *He believed.*

8. **A** In this sentence, it seems that the bird is doing the gazing. To correct the dangling participle, change *gazing* to *When I gazed.*

9. **E**   Choices (A), (B), (C), and (D) are all correct.

10. **A**   The word *neither* should be followed by *nor*.

11. **C**   Wrong pronoun. The relative pronoun used to refer to people is *who*; *which* can only refer to things.

12. **E**   Choices (A), (B), (C), and (D) are all correct.

13. **C**   Error in diction. The correct word is *imply*, which means to hint or suggest.

14. **E**   Choices (A), (B), (C), and (D) are all correct.

15. **C**   Error in case. The noun immediately preceding a gerund should be in the possessive case. Change to *burglar's*.

16. **B**   Omission of an important word in the comparison. Change *as good* to *as good as*.

17. **A**   Error in case. The subject of the verb *abandoned* must be in the nominative case. Change *him* to *he*.

18. **C**   Double negative. The word *but*, meaning except, conveys a negative meaning. Therefore, the use of the negative verb *wasn't going* is redundant. The verb should be *was going*.

19. **C**   This is a run-on sentence. It may be corrected by changing the comma to a semicolon, or by breaking the sentence into two sentences after the word *rocks*.

20. **D**   Lack of parallel structure. Change *and the work of the Continental Congress* to *and how the Continental Congress worked*.

21. **C**   Misuse of the transitive verb *raise* when the intransitive verb *rise* should be used. Since the verb in this clause does not have an object, an intransitive verb is required. Change *raise* to *rise*.

22. **B**   Error in diction. *Healthful* is the correct word to describe climate. Change *healthier* to *more healthful*.

23. **C**   Squinting modifier. Does the sentence state that the operation must be done within a year or that the patient has less than a year before going blind? As written, the meaning is ambiguous. Move *within a year* to the end of the sentence.

24. **C**   Lack of agreement between subject and verb. Change the verb *were equipped* to *was equipped* to agree with the singular subject *one*.

25. **E**   Choices (A), (B), (C), and (D) are all correct.

26. **C**   This sentence illustrates the use of the future perfect tense. The present perfect tense, as used in choice (A), and the past perfect tense, as used in choice (B), are incorrect. Choice (C) correctly indicates that an anticipated event will be completed before a definite time in the future. Choice (D) is weak because of the use of the passive voice and the consequent vagueness as to who is performing the action. Choice (E) is awkward because of the needless separation of subject (*we*) from verb (*shall have traveled*).

27. **D**   Choices (A) and (C) are examples of run-on sentences. Choices (C) and (D) correct the run-on sentence. Choice (C), however, confuses the meanings of *complementary* and *complimentary*. Choice (E) leaves the verb *is not* without a subject.

28. **E**   In choices (A) and (B) we find an unwarranted shift from the third person pronoun *one* to the second person pronoun *you*. Choices (C) and (D) improperly use *affect* instead of *effect*.

29. **D**   Choices (A) and (B) illustrate the incorrect use of *due to*. The change to *inasmuch as* in choice (C) creates a sentence fragment. Choice (E) is poor because it omits the causal relationship implied by the original sentence.

30. **E**   Choices (A) and (B) improperly use the present perfect tense. In choice (C) we find an unnecessary separation of the noun (*explanation*) and its modifier (*of her mysterious ailment*). Choice (D) changes the meaning of the original sentence.

31. **A**   Choices (C) and (D) create run-on sentences. Choice (B) changes the meaning of the sentence. Choice (E) makes an unwarranted shift to the passive voice, resulting in a vague and awkward sentence.

32. **D**   Choices (A) and (B) violate parallel structure. Choices (C) and (E) change the meaning of the original sentence.

33. **B**   The *if* clause with which the sentence begins expresses a condition contrary to fact and therefore requires the subjunctive mood. Choice (B) provides the necessary subjunctive. Choice (C) changes the meaning of the sentence.

34. **B**   Choices (A), (D), and (E) compare two things which cannot be directly compared—subways and cities. In choice (C), the omission of *other* changes the meaning of the sentence.

35. **D**   Choices (A), (B) and (E) omit important parts of the verb. *Hopefully* in choices (C) and (E) is wrong; although many people use it this way, most grammarians do not accept it as a substitute for *we hope*. (Strictly speaking, *hopefully* should only be used to mean *in a hopeful way*, as in *The farmer searched the skies hopefully looking for signs of rain*.)

36. **E**   Choice (A) has a dangling participle. Choices (B), (C), and (D) change the meaning of the sentence.

37. **A**   *Being that* in choices (B) and (E) is nonstandard and therefore incorrect. Choices (C) and (D) make slight changes in the meaning of the sentence.

38. **B**   Choice (A) contains a misplaced modifier. Was the flight attendant partially defrosted? So choice (A) would imply. In choices (C) and (D), the word *only* should come immediately before *partially*. In choice (E), the transitive verb *served* does not have an object.

39. **B**   Choices (A), (C), (D) and (E) suffer from the lack of agreement between the pronouns *they* and *them* (plural) and their antecedent *anyone* (singular).

40. **D**   The comma in choices (B), (C), and (E) creates a run-on sentence. In choices (A) and (B), the demonstrative adjective *these* (plural) does not agree with the noun it modifies, *kind* (singular). Choice (D) corrects both errors.

41. **D**   Lack of parallel structure. The change from an adverb (*intelligently*) to an adverbial phrase (*with clarity and skill*) is unnecessary and clumsy. Change the sentence to *The young orator spoke intelligently, clearly, and skillfully about her subject*.

42. **C**   Lack of agreement between the singular subject *the variety* and the plural verb *are*. Change *are* to *is*.

43. **C**   Same as question 42. Change *are* to *is*.

44. **E**   Choices (A), (B), (C), and (D) are all correct.

45. **B**   The correct form in this sentence is *all together*.

46. **C**   The antecedent of the pronoun *which* is the noun *schools* (plural). Therefore, it requires a plural verb. Change *has been* to *have been*.

47. **A**   The subjunctive verb *had been* is required in a clause describing a condition contrary to fact.

48. **D**   Change *me* to *I*. The elliptical clause is *than I (finished the course)*.

49. **E**   Choices (A), (B), (C), and (D) are all correct.

50. **C**   The objective complement of an infinitive is in the objective case. Change *he* to *him*.

answer sheet—typical test c

To the student:

Take the following test under examination conditions.

Have on hand a supply of #2 pencils and a good eraser.

Limit yourself to thirty minutes.

Because you will be penalized for wrong answers, do not guess wildly. However, if you can eliminate some of the choices, you can improve your score by guessing.

The answer grid below is provided for your convenience. Fill in the oval which contains the letter of your choice. You may remove this page from the book for ease in marking your answers.

1. Ⓐ Ⓑ Ⓒ Ⓓ Ⓔ
2. Ⓐ Ⓑ Ⓒ Ⓓ Ⓔ
3. Ⓐ Ⓑ Ⓒ Ⓓ Ⓔ
4. Ⓐ Ⓑ Ⓒ Ⓓ Ⓔ
5. Ⓐ Ⓑ Ⓒ Ⓓ Ⓔ
6. Ⓐ Ⓑ Ⓒ Ⓓ Ⓔ
7. Ⓐ Ⓑ Ⓒ Ⓓ Ⓔ
8. Ⓐ Ⓑ Ⓒ Ⓓ Ⓔ
9. Ⓐ Ⓑ Ⓒ Ⓓ Ⓔ
10. Ⓐ Ⓑ Ⓒ Ⓓ Ⓔ
11. Ⓐ Ⓑ Ⓒ Ⓓ Ⓔ
12. Ⓐ Ⓑ Ⓒ Ⓓ Ⓔ
13. Ⓐ Ⓑ Ⓒ Ⓓ Ⓔ

14. Ⓐ Ⓑ Ⓒ Ⓓ Ⓔ
15. Ⓐ Ⓑ Ⓒ Ⓓ Ⓔ
16. Ⓐ Ⓑ Ⓒ Ⓓ Ⓔ
17. Ⓐ Ⓑ Ⓒ Ⓓ Ⓔ
18. Ⓐ Ⓑ Ⓒ Ⓓ Ⓔ
19. Ⓐ Ⓑ Ⓒ Ⓓ Ⓔ
20. Ⓐ Ⓑ Ⓒ Ⓓ Ⓔ
21. Ⓐ Ⓑ Ⓒ Ⓓ Ⓔ
22. Ⓐ Ⓑ Ⓒ Ⓓ Ⓔ
23. Ⓐ Ⓑ Ⓒ Ⓓ Ⓔ
24. Ⓐ Ⓑ Ⓒ Ⓓ Ⓔ
25. Ⓐ Ⓑ Ⓒ Ⓓ Ⓔ
26. Ⓐ Ⓑ Ⓒ Ⓓ Ⓔ

27. Ⓐ Ⓑ Ⓒ Ⓓ Ⓔ
28. Ⓐ Ⓑ Ⓒ Ⓓ Ⓔ
29. Ⓐ Ⓑ Ⓒ Ⓓ Ⓔ
30. Ⓐ Ⓑ Ⓒ Ⓓ Ⓔ
31. Ⓐ Ⓑ Ⓒ Ⓓ Ⓔ
32. Ⓐ Ⓑ Ⓒ Ⓓ Ⓔ
33. Ⓐ Ⓑ Ⓒ Ⓓ Ⓔ
34. Ⓐ Ⓑ Ⓒ Ⓓ Ⓔ
35. Ⓐ Ⓑ Ⓒ Ⓓ Ⓔ
36. Ⓐ Ⓑ Ⓒ Ⓓ Ⓔ
37. Ⓐ Ⓑ Ⓒ Ⓓ Ⓔ
38. Ⓐ Ⓑ Ⓒ Ⓓ Ⓔ
39. Ⓐ Ⓑ Ⓒ Ⓓ Ⓔ

40. Ⓐ Ⓑ Ⓒ Ⓓ Ⓔ
41. Ⓐ Ⓑ Ⓒ Ⓓ Ⓔ
42. Ⓐ Ⓑ Ⓒ Ⓓ Ⓔ
43. Ⓐ Ⓑ Ⓒ Ⓓ Ⓔ
44. Ⓐ Ⓑ Ⓒ Ⓓ Ⓔ
45. Ⓐ Ⓑ Ⓒ Ⓓ Ⓔ
46. Ⓐ Ⓑ Ⓒ Ⓓ Ⓔ
47. Ⓐ Ⓑ Ⓒ Ⓓ Ⓔ
48. Ⓐ Ⓑ Ⓒ Ⓓ Ⓔ
49. Ⓐ Ⓑ Ⓒ Ⓓ Ⓔ
50. Ⓐ Ⓑ Ⓒ Ⓓ Ⓔ

chapter 9

typical test c

Time: 30 minutes   50 questions

Directions: In each of the sentences below, there are four underlined words or phrases. If you think there is an error in usage, grammar, diction, or punctuation in one of the underlined parts, write the letter indicated on your answer paper. If there is no error in any of the underlined parts, mark (E) on your answer paper.

Example: The aircraft carrier with all her accompanying ships are going to sail to the
   A   B   C

Persian Gulf. No error
   D   E
The correct answer is (C).

---

1. When Sam Feldman comes back
      A
   from his sales trips, he usually
                  B
   submitted his expense account to
      C   D
   the chief bookkeeper. No error
                         E

2. The variety of gourmet foods in
                    A
   this delicatessen are
                     B
   exceptionally large for such a
                    C
   small establishment. No error
      D   E

3. After many hours of questioning,
                     A
   the police had a clear picture of
                B
   the crime and released all
   suspects but he and Harry.
                  C   D
   No error
      E

4. The dying plants in the
   overcrowded chapel made us feel
      A   B
   sick because they smelled sickly
      C   D
   sweet. No error
          E

5. In the opinion of many who
   <u>A</u>
   witnessed the dispute, there
   <u>B</u>
   was never any doubts about
   <u>C</u>   <u>D</u>
   the identity of the instigator of

   the quarrel. No error
                    <u>E</u>

6. Mrs. Rivera scolded her students
                    <u>A</u>
   for creating a disturbance during
                    <u>B</u>   <u>C</u>
   recess and how they cheated on
                    <u>D</u>
   the examination. No error
                    <u>E</u>

7. Had I been aware of the dire
   <u>A</u>   <u>B</u>
   consequences of our actions, I
                    <u>C</u>
   might not have participated in
                    <u>D</u>
   the student rally. No error
                    <u>E</u>

8. Smallpox has been eliminated as
                    <u>A</u>
   a scourge of mankind, but others
   <u>B</u>   <u>C</u>
   must still be wiped out. No error
                    <u>D</u>   <u>E</u>

9. Me talking at the meeting was a
   <u>A</u>
   surprise to everyone, including
                    <u>B</u>
   myself, because I am usually a
   <u>C</u>   <u>D</u>
   very shy and reticent individual.

   No error
   <u>E</u>

10. When the ophthalmologist
    <u>A</u>
    examined my eyes, she found
    <u>B</u>
    that my left eye was

    most efficient and that I was not
    <u>C</u>
    using my right eye as fully as I
                    <u>D</u>
    should. No error
                    <u>E</u>

11. After listening to our accounts of
    <u>A</u>
    the automobile accident, the

    policeman said, "Either you or
    <u>B</u>   <u>C</u>
    the lady are not telling the truth."
                    <u>D</u>

    No error
    <u>E</u>

12. The hospital administrator

    as well as the physicians are
    <u>A</u>   <u>B</u>
    eagerly awaiting the arrival of the
    <u>C</u>
    new dialysis equipment. No error
    <u>D</u>   <u>E</u>

13. Didn't you realize that it was me
                    <u>A</u>   <u>B</u> <u>C</u>
    on the telephone pretending to
                    <u>D</u>
    be your uncle? No error
                    <u>E</u>

14. If both you and John want to be
    <u>A</u>   <u>B</u>
    school valedictorian, then either

    you or John is going
    <u>C</u>
    to be disappointed. No error
    <u>D</u>   <u>E</u>

15. When we reached the scene of
                    <u>A</u>
    the accident, we became

    nauseated because we
    <u>B</u>
    couldn't hardly stand the sight
    <u>C</u>
    of so much carnage. No error
    <u>D</u>   <u>E</u>

16. Neither the geologists or the
                    <u>A</u>
    mining engineers previously
    <u>B</u>
    suspected the existence of fossil
                    <u>C</u>
    fuels in this mountainous region.
                    <u>D</u>
    No error
    <u>E</u>

17. His voice is very aggravating; it is
    <u>A</u>   <u>B</u>
    harsh and grates on my nerves.
    <u>C</u>   <u>D</u>
    No error
    <u>E</u>

18. Despite the inclement weather,
    —A—
    John and his swimming coach

    are going to try to swim around
    —B—   —C—   —D—
    Manhattan Island. No error
                        —E—

19. After the visitor signed the
    —A—
    historic guest book, which held
    —B—
    the signatures of the great and

    near-great who had visited the
    —C—   —D—
    manor during the past fifty years.

    No error
    —E—

20. We were delayed in traffic; by the
       —A—
    time I reached the employment
              —B—
    agency, the job was taken by
                  —C—
    someone else. No error
    —D—   —E—

21. Mathematics and how to read
    —————A—————
    and write are subjects
    ————— —B—
    which must be mastered by
            —C—
    anyone eager to advance himself
    —D—
    in this world. No error
                  —E—

22. The noise at the airport

    was deafening which made
    —A—   —B—
    conversation difficult, if not
                 —C—
    impossible. No error
    —D—   —E—

23. This building seems to be
    —A—   —B—
    as large or larger than the Eiffel
    —C—   —D—
    Tower in Paris. No error
                   —E—

24. Drinking wine and cocktails all
    —A—
    evening, there was bound to be
                 —B—
    an automobile accident when

    they started going home. No error
                 —C— —D—   —E—

25. The dramatic events of the past
                              —A—
    few weeks will affect us
                 —B—
    for years to come, because they
    —C—
    have changed the very basis of

    our nation's economy. No error
    —D—   —E—

Directions: In each sentence below, some or all of the words are underlined. The portion underlined may be correct or it may contain an error in grammar, diction, style, or punctuation. The sentence is followed by five possible ways of writing the underlined portion. If you think the underlined portion is correct in the original sentence, you will choose (A) as your answer, because (A) repeats the underlined section. If you think the underlined portion is incorrect, you will select the group of words from choices (B), (C), (D) or (E) which best corrects the error you have found. Do not select a choice which changes the meaning of the original sentence.

Example: Although I calculate that he will be here any minute, I cannot wait much longer for him to arrive.

    (A)   Although I calculate that he will be here

    (B)   Although I reckon that he will be here

    (C)   Because I calculate that he will be here

    (D)   Although I am confident that he will be here

    (E)   Because I am confident that he will be here

The correct answer is (D).

---

26.   Today, more than sixty years after women won the right to vote, they are concerned with the problem of the equal rights amendment, which cause has been opposed by many men and women.

    (A)   which cause has been opposed by many men and women

    (B)   and this cause has been opposed by many men and women

    (C)   which cause is being opposed by many

    (D)   a cause opposed by many men and women

    (E)   and many men and women have opposed it

27.   The word processor has revolutionized office procedures more than any machine of modern times.

    (A)   more than any machine

    (B)   more than has any machine

    (C)   more than any other machine

    (D)   more than has any other machine

    (E)   more than any other machine has

28.   Before starting a program of diet and exercise, a consultation with your physician is advisable.

    (A)   a consultation with your physician is advisable

    (B)   it is advisable to get a consultation with your physician

    (C)   a physician's consultation is advisable

    (D)   a consultation with your physician is necessary

    (E)   you should consult your physician

29. A late entry in the race, Dashing Spirit surprised everyone, <u>he led</u> from wire to wire.

    (A)   he led

    (B)   for he led

    (C)   with him leading

    (D)   which led

    (E)   he was in front

30. If I <u>had taken the time to read</u> the assignment, I would not have failed the test the teacher gave us this morning.

    (A)   had taken the time to read

    (B)   would have taken the time to read

    (C)   had taken the time to have read

    (D)   took the time to read

    (E)   had took the time to read

31. As one follows this <u>program of exercise and relaxation, you get</u> a feeling of well-being which is very exhilarating.

    (A)   As one follows this program of exercise and relaxation, you get

    (B)   If one follows this exercise and relaxation program, you get

    (C)   As you follow this program of exercise and relaxation, you will get

    (D)   After you follow this program of exercise and relaxation, you will have gotten

    (E)   As you follow this program of exercise and relaxation, you will have gotten

32. <u>Being that only twenty-four states have ratified</u> the proposed amendment, we can assume that it will not be adopted.

    (A)   Being that only twenty-four states have ratified

    (B)   Since twenty-four states only have ratified

    (C)   Being as only twenty-four states have ratified

    (D)   Inasmuch as only twenty-four states have ratified

    (E)   Inasmuch as twenty-four states have only ratified

33. <u>Everyone but Harry and me handed in his homework.</u>

    (A)   Everyone but Harry and me handed in his homework.

    (B)   Everyone but Harry and me handed in their homework.

    (C)   Everyone but Harry and I handed in their homework.

    (D)   Everyone but Harry and I handed in his homework.

    (E)   All but Harry and I handed in their homework.

34. I have studied the works of George Bernard Shaw not only for their plots <u>but also because they are very witty.</u>

    (A)   but also because they are very witty

    (B)   but because they are also very witty

    (C)   but for their wit also

    (D)   but because they are very witty also

    (E)   but also for their wit

35. Some resemblances can be found, however, and should cause some moments of anxiety to the present administration.

    (A) Some resemblances can be found, however, and
    (B) Some resemblances can be found; however, and
    (C) Some resemblances can be found, however; and
    (D) Some resemblances which can be found, however, and
    (E) Some resemblances can be found. However, which

36. In 1896, Henri Bequerel found that uranium salts emitted penetrating radiations similar to those which Roentgen produced only a year earlier with a gas discharge tube.

    (A) similar to those which Roentgen produced
    (B) like to those which Roentgen produced
    (C) like those which Roentgen had produced
    (D) similar to them that Roentgen produced
    (E) similar to those Roentgen produced

37. The proposed cuts in the welfare programs are going to hurt the poor; they will have no place to go for relief.

    (A) the poor; they will have
    (B) the poor being that they will have
    (C) the poor, which will have
    (D) the poor, they will have
    (E) the poor, he will have

38. The speaker had scarcely started to speak when a shot was fired and the audience began to run for the exits.

    (A) when a shot was fired
    (B) when he fired a shot
    (C) than a shot was fired
    (D) than he fired a shot
    (E) than a shot had been fired

39. Revered by all who knew him, loyal followers were always at the leader's side.

    (A) loyal followers were always at the leader's side
    (B) his loyal followers were always at the leader's side
    (C) the leader with his loyal followers at his side
    (D) the leader always had his loyal followers at his side
    (E) the leader's loyal followers were always at his side

40. I had ought to carefully question you about this.

    (A) had ought to carefully question you
    (B) ought to question you carefully
    (C) carefully ought to have questioned you
    (D) had ought to have carefully questioned you
    (E) ought carefully to have questioned you

Directions: In each of the sentences below, there are four underlined words or phrases. If you think there is an error in usage, grammar, diction, or punctuation in any of the underlined parts, write the letter indicated on your answer paper. If there is no error in any of the underlined parts, mark (E) on your answer paper.

Example: The aircraft carrier with all her accompanying ships are going to sail to the
A   B   C

Persian Gulf. No error
D   E
The correct answer is (C).

---

41. Losing much time when the
 A
 typewriter had to be repaired, my
         B
 worries about not being able
        C
 to meet the deadline increased.
 D
 No error
 E

42. Because we had to buy
 A
 provisions for the trip, pack our

 gear, and stow it in the car, it

 wasn't until late afternoon that
     B   C
 we were already to start. No error
       D   E

43. This present from John and
          A
 she came as a surprise
   B
 because I thought they
       C
 had been displeased by our
         D
 absence from their party.

 No error
    E

44. Do not squander your
       A
 inheritance, but try to live on the
           B
 interest which the principal
     C   D
 provides. No error
        E

45. In her candid autobiography, the
       A
 author discusses her early years,
             B
 her desire to become an actress,
           C

and how she made her debut on
          D
 the stage. No error
        E

46. Last week I thought we ought
         A
 to have tried out for the school
      B   C
 play; today I am glad we
           D
 refused. No error
       E

47. Although I do not like
     A
 this kind of a book, I am going to
       B
 read it because I think it

 will impress my teacher when
      C   D
 I report on it. No error
         E

48. If John had realized the
 A   B
 consequences of his actions, he

 would have behaved differently.
         C   D
 No error
   E

49. In contrast to the beauty of the
           A
 park was the filth in the streets
   B
 and the dilapidated condition of
           C
 the surrounding buildings.
          D
 No error
   E

50. I have not and never will
      A   B
 complain about the grades I
        C
 receive; I let my parents do the

 complaining. No error
      D   E

STOP
END OF TYPICAL TEST C

Answer Key—Typical Test C

1. **C**	11. **D**	21. **A**	31. **C**	41. **A**
2. **B**	12. **B**	22. **B**	32. **D**	42. **D**
3. **C**	13. **C**	23. **C**	33. **A**	43. **B**
4. **E**	14. **E**	24. **A**	34. **E**	44. **E**
5. **C**	15. **C**	25. **E**	35. **A**	45. **D**
6. **D**	16. **A**	26. **D**	36. **C**	46. **B**
7. **E**	17. **B**	27. **C**	37. **A**	47. **B**
8. **C**	18. **E**	28. **E**	38. **A**	48. **E**
9. **A**	19. **A**	29. **B**	39. **D**	49. **B**
10. **C**	20. **C**	30. **A**	40. **B**	50. **A**

Item Classification Chart—Typical Test C

Error	Question	See Page
Fragment	19	47, 75
Run-on	29	75
Subject-verb Agreement	2, 5, 11, 12, 49	76
Pronoun-Antecedent Agreement		
Pronoun Reference	8, 22, 26, 31	56
Case	3, 9, 13, 43	27, 54, 76
Unclear Placement of Modifier	28	58, 59
Dangling Modifier	24, 39, 41	59, 77
Parallel Structure	6, 21, 34, 45	60, 77
Sequence of Tenses	1, 20, 36, 46	57
Mood		
Verb Conjugation	40, 50	30
Transitive – Intransitive Verbs		
Adjective Comparison	10, 23, 27	43, 76
Adjective–Adverb Confusion		
Double Negative	15	62
Diction	16, 17, 32, 42, 47	77
Idiomatic Expression		
No Error in Question	4, 7, 14, 18, 25, 30, 33, 35, 37, 38, 44, 48	

How Well Did You Do on Typical Test C?

1. Find your raw score.

    a. Count the number of correct answers.

    b. Count the number of incorrect answers. (Do not count blanks as incorrect answers.)

    c. Use this formula to find your raw score:

    Raw Score = Number Correct − ¼ Number Incorrect

    Example: A student answers 41 questions correctly. He answers seven incorrectly and leaves two questions unanswered. His raw score is 41 − 1.75 (one-fourth of 7) which equals 39.25.

2. Evaluate your raw score.

Raw Score	Evaluation
45 to 50	Superior
39 to 44	Above average
33 to 38	Average
15 to 32	May need remedial work in college
Below 15	Definitely needs remedial work

How Can You Profit from This Test?

1. Look at the explanation of answers which follows this page. Notice the areas where you made your errors.

2. Chapters 3–5 of this book contain a review of the important elements of grammar, diction, style, and punctuation covered in this test. Study the sections which discuss the areas where you made your errors. If you scored low on this test, you should review all three chapters.

3. Go on to Typical Test D.

Answers Explained—Typical Test C

1. **C** Faulty sequence of tenses. The use of the present tense *comes* conflicts with the use of the past tense *submitted.* Therefore, *submitted* should be changed to *submits.*

2. **D** Error in agreement between subject and verb. The phrase *the variety* calls for the singular verb *is* instead of *are.*

3. **C** Error in the case of the pronoun. *But,* as used in this sentence, is a preposition meaning except. It should be followed by the objective case pronoun *him.*

4. **E**   All four choices are correct.

5. **C**   Error in agreement between subject and verb. *Doubts,* a plural subject, requires the plural verb *were.*

6. **D**   Lack of parallel structure. Change *how they cheated* to *for cheating,* to match the structure of *for creating.*

7. **E**   All four choices are correct.

8. **C**   Unclear reference of pronoun. Change *others* to *other diseases.*

9. **A**   Error in the case of the pronoun. A noun or pronoun immediately preceding a gerund should be in the possessive case. Change *me* to *my,* since it precedes the gerund *talking.*

10. **C**   Error in comparison of adjectives. When only two things are being compared, the comparative form should be used, not the superlative. Change *most efficient* to *more efficient.*

11. **D**   Error in agreement. In an *either . . . or* construction, the verb agrees with the noun or pronoun that follows *or.* Change *are* to *is* to agree with the singular noun *lady.*

12. **B**   Error in agreement of subject and verb. The subject *administrator* is singular, and should be followed by the singular verb *is.*

13. **C**   Error in case. The copulative verb *to be* should be followed by a predicate nominative. Change *me* to *I.*

14. **E**   All four choices are correct.

15. **C**   Avoid the double negative *couldn't hardly.* Remember, the word *hardly* should be considered negative in meaning. Change to *could hardly.*

16. **A**   Error in diction. The word *neither* should always be followed by *nor.*

17. **B**   Error in diction. *Aggravating* should not be used as a substitute for *irritating* or *annoying;* to aggravate is to worsen.

18. **E**   All four choices are correct.

19. **A**   This is a sentence fragment because it does not have an independent clause. The deletion of the word *after* will change the dependent clause to an independent or principal clause.

20. **C**   Error in sequence of tenses. The past perfect tense *had been taken* should be used to indicate that the taking of the job occurred prior to the time I reached the agency.

21. **A**   Lack of parallel structure. Change *Mathematics and how to read and write* to *Mathematics, reading, and writing.*

22. **B**   Poor reference of pronoun. *Which* refers to the entire sentence rather than to a specific antecedent. Change the sentence to *The noise at the airport was deafening; this made . . .*

23. **C**   Omission of an important word. To complete the comparison and maintain clarity in the sentence, change *as large* to *as large as.*

24. **A**   *Drinking* is a dangling participle, because it has nothing to modify in the sentence. One way of correcting this error is to convert the phrase to a subordinate clause: *Because they had been drinking wine and cocktails all evening . . .*

25. **E**   All four choices are correct.

26. **D**   The underlined portion can be better expressed as *a cause opposed by many men and women.* Choice (D) corrects the awkward word order found in choice (A) and the misused tense in choice (C). The use of *and* in choices (B) and (E) changes the meaning of the sentence by elevating a subordinate idea to a main or principal idea.

27. **C**   Choices (A) and (B) contain a faulty comparison. The word processor *is* a modern machine, and so the word *other* must be included. In choices (D) and (E), the word *has* is unnecessary and awkward; it can easily be understood.

28. **E**   Choice (E) best indicates the doer of the action in the sentence.

29. **B**   The inclusion of the conjunction *for* eliminates the run-on sentence found in choices (A) and (E).

30. **A**   The past perfect subjunctive tense is needed in an *if* clause followed by a *would have* clause. The past tense of the infinitive *to have read* in choice (C) is incorrect.

31. **C** The switch from *one* to *you* in choices (A) and (B) is incorrect. Choices (D) and (E) have errors in the tense of the verb.

32. **D** *Being that* in choices (A) and (C) is incorrect. The placement of *only* in choices (B) and (E) is incorrect.

33. **A** As used in this sentence, *but* is a preposition meaning *except* and, as such, requires the objective case *me*. Choices (C), (D), and (E) are, therefore, incorrect. In choice (B), the antecedent of the plural pronoun *their* is the singular word *everyone*. To make choice (B) correct, *their* should be changed to *his*.

34. **E** Parallel structure is violated in choices (A), (B), and (D). The placement of *also* in choice (C) is poor, for it ends the sentence on an anticlimactic note.

35. **A** Choice (B) is incorrect, because the semicolon and *and* should not be used together. In choice (C), the semicolon should precede *however*. The use of *which* in choice (D) makes the sentence a dependent clause, and therefore a fragment. In choice (E), the second group of words, beginning with *However*, is a sentence fragment.

36. **C** The past perfect tense *had produced* is required in this sentence to show that Roentgen's work preceded that of Bequerel.

37. **A** In choice (B), *being that* is incorrect. In choices (D) and (E), the use of the comma creates a run-on sentence; in addition, the singular pronoun *he* in choice (E) is incorrect. In choice (C), the pronoun *which* is wrong; it should only be used to refer to things, not people.

38. **A** The correct idiom is *scarcely . . . when*. Choice (B) changes the meaning of the sentence.

39. **D** Choices (A), (B), and (E) leave the dangling participle *revered* dangling. Choice (C) results in a sentence fragment.

40. **B** *Ought* can be used only as an auxiliary verb. It does not change to form different tenses. Therefore, *had ought* in choices (A) and (D) is incorrect. The past infinitive *to have questioned* should not follow *ought*; therefore, choices (C) and (E) are wrong.

41. **A** *Losing* is a dangling participle because it cannot modify *worries*. To correct the sentence, *losing* should be changed to a phrase such as *when I lost*.

42. **D** *All ready* is the correct form in this sentence.

43. **B** Error in case. The pronoun *she* is the object of the preposition *from*. Change *she* to *her*.

44. **E** All four choices are correct.

45. **D** Lack of parallel structure. Delete the phrase *how she made* to retain parallel structure.

46. **B** The auxiliary verb *ought* should be followed by the present tense of the infinitive. Change *to have tried out* to *to try out*.

47. **B** The article *a* is unnecessary in this kind of phrase. Delete it.

48. **E** All four choices are correct.

49. **B** Lack of agreement between subject and verb. *Filth* and *condition* form a compound subject, which calls for a plural verb. Change *was* to *were*.

50. **A** Improper omission of part of the verb. The sentence should read *I have not complained and never will complain*.

answer sheet–typical test d

To the student:

Take the following test under examination conditions.

Have on hand a supply of #2 pencils and a good eraser.

Limit yourself to thirty minutes.

Because you will be penalized for wrong answers, do not guess wildly. However, if you can eliminate some of the choices, you can improve your score by guessing.

The answer grid below is provided for your convenience. Fill in the oval which contains the letter of your choice. You may remove this page from the book for ease in marking your answers.

1. Ⓐ Ⓑ Ⓒ Ⓓ Ⓔ   14. Ⓐ Ⓑ Ⓒ Ⓓ Ⓔ   27. Ⓐ Ⓑ Ⓒ Ⓓ Ⓔ   40. Ⓐ Ⓑ Ⓒ Ⓓ Ⓔ
2. Ⓐ Ⓑ Ⓒ Ⓓ Ⓔ   15. Ⓐ Ⓑ Ⓒ Ⓓ Ⓔ   28. Ⓐ Ⓑ Ⓒ Ⓓ Ⓔ   41. Ⓐ Ⓑ Ⓒ Ⓓ Ⓔ
3. Ⓐ Ⓑ Ⓒ Ⓓ Ⓔ   16. Ⓐ Ⓑ Ⓒ Ⓓ Ⓔ   29. Ⓐ Ⓑ Ⓒ Ⓓ Ⓔ   42. Ⓐ Ⓑ Ⓒ Ⓓ Ⓔ
4. Ⓐ Ⓑ Ⓒ Ⓓ Ⓔ   17. Ⓐ Ⓑ Ⓒ Ⓓ Ⓔ   30. Ⓐ Ⓑ Ⓒ Ⓓ Ⓔ   43. Ⓐ Ⓑ Ⓒ Ⓓ Ⓔ
5. Ⓐ Ⓑ Ⓒ Ⓓ Ⓔ   18. Ⓐ Ⓑ Ⓒ Ⓓ Ⓔ   31. Ⓐ Ⓑ Ⓒ Ⓓ Ⓔ   44. Ⓐ Ⓑ Ⓒ Ⓓ Ⓔ
6. Ⓐ Ⓑ Ⓒ Ⓓ Ⓔ   19. Ⓐ Ⓑ Ⓒ Ⓓ Ⓔ   32. Ⓐ Ⓑ Ⓒ Ⓓ Ⓔ   45. Ⓐ Ⓑ Ⓒ Ⓓ Ⓔ
7. Ⓐ Ⓑ Ⓒ Ⓓ Ⓔ   20. Ⓐ Ⓑ Ⓒ Ⓓ Ⓔ   33. Ⓐ Ⓑ Ⓒ Ⓓ Ⓔ   46. Ⓐ Ⓑ Ⓒ Ⓓ Ⓔ
8. Ⓐ Ⓑ Ⓒ Ⓓ Ⓔ   21. Ⓐ Ⓑ Ⓒ Ⓓ Ⓔ   34. Ⓐ Ⓑ Ⓒ Ⓓ Ⓔ   47. Ⓐ Ⓑ Ⓒ Ⓓ Ⓔ
9. Ⓐ Ⓑ Ⓒ Ⓓ Ⓔ   22. Ⓐ Ⓑ Ⓒ Ⓓ Ⓔ   35. Ⓐ Ⓑ Ⓒ Ⓓ Ⓔ   48. Ⓐ Ⓑ Ⓒ Ⓓ Ⓔ
10. Ⓐ Ⓑ Ⓒ Ⓓ Ⓔ   23. Ⓐ Ⓑ Ⓒ Ⓓ Ⓔ   36. Ⓐ Ⓑ Ⓒ Ⓓ Ⓔ   49. Ⓐ Ⓑ Ⓒ Ⓓ Ⓔ
11. Ⓐ Ⓑ Ⓒ Ⓓ Ⓔ   24. Ⓐ Ⓑ Ⓒ Ⓓ Ⓔ   37. Ⓐ Ⓑ Ⓒ Ⓓ Ⓔ   50. Ⓐ Ⓑ Ⓒ Ⓓ Ⓔ
12. Ⓐ Ⓑ Ⓒ Ⓓ Ⓔ   25. Ⓐ Ⓑ Ⓒ Ⓓ Ⓔ   38. Ⓐ Ⓑ Ⓒ Ⓓ Ⓔ
13. Ⓐ Ⓑ Ⓒ Ⓓ Ⓔ   26. Ⓐ Ⓑ Ⓒ Ⓓ Ⓔ   39. Ⓐ Ⓑ Ⓒ Ⓓ Ⓔ

chapter 10

typical test d

Time: 30 minutes

50 questions

Directions: In each of the sentences below, there are four underlined words or phrases. If you think there is an error in usage, grammar, diction, or punctuation in any of the underlined parts, write the letter indicated on your answer paper. If there is no error in any of the underlined parts, mark (E) on your answer paper.

Example: The aircraft carrier with all her accompanying ships are going to sail to the
A   B   C

Persian Gulf. No error
D   E
The correct answer is (C).

---

1. Not one of the Thompson boys

   have his father's athletic ability or
   A   B   C
   the desire to follow in his
   D
   footsteps. No error
   E

2. The advertisement announced
   A
   that a reward of $5000 would be

   given to whomever provided
   B   C
   information leading to the arrest
   D
   and conviction of the arsonists.

   No error
   E

3. I was real angry when I learned
   A   B
   that some of the jurors in this
   C
   trial had been bribed by the
   D
   defendant's associates. No error
   E

4. Rushing through the woods, I
   A
   was impeded by the hanging
   B   C
   branches and the lush weeds

   which covered the forest bed.
   D
   No error
   E

5. Sam <u>has made up</u> all the
   A
   assignments he <u>missed</u> when he
   B
   was sick, and he <u>has brung</u> them
   C
   <u>in to</u> the teacher. <u>No error</u>
   DE

6. <u>Chasing</u> after the car, the
   A
   <u>speeding</u> vehicle soon
   B
   <u>outdistanced</u> my <u>excited</u> dog.
   CD
   <u>No error</u>
   E

7. The collection of butterflies in
   the Science Museum <u>are</u>
   A
   <u>very valuable</u> and irreplaceable
   B
   <u>if lost</u>, stolen, <u>or destroyed</u>.
   CD
   <u>No error</u>
   E

8. Eric <u>will be remembered</u> for his
   A
   <u>ability</u> to play baseball, to run the
   B
   <u>hundred-yard dash</u>, and
   C
   <u>he could swim</u>. <u>No error</u>
   DE

9. <u>Because</u> we are on the honor
   A
   system, we <u>had ought</u> to report
   B
   the <u>flagrant</u> cheating that
   C
   <u>went on</u> in the examination
   D
   room. <u>No error</u>
   E

10. <u>Between</u> John and <u>me</u>, <u>there</u> is a
    ABC
    feeling of mutual understanding
    <u>which</u> works to our advantage.
    D
    <u>No error</u>
    E

11. We <u>were not prepared</u> for the <u>last</u>
    AB
    blackout; there <u>wasn't</u> scarcely
    C

    any candles in the house.
    D
    <u>No error</u>
    E

12. I <u>paid</u> my gas bill on March 22
    A
    and my telephone bill <u>on March</u>
    B
    27, but I did <u>not</u> receive a receipt
    C
    for <u>either</u> payment. <u>No error</u>
    DE

13. There <u>is</u>, <u>in</u> this difficult situation,
    AB
    <u>only</u> two ways to <u>react</u>—resist or
    CD
    surrender. <u>No error</u>
    E

14. <u>While</u> <u>visiting my aunt</u>
    AB
    in Los Angeles
    <u>at the request of my children</u> I
    C
    went to Disneyland. <u>No error</u>
    DE

15. The roses we <u>planted</u> five years
    A
    ago are <u>more lovelier</u> today <u>than</u>
    BC
    in <u>past</u> years. <u>No error</u>
    DE

16. When I <u>attended</u> the trial, I was
    A
    <u>prejudiced</u>; I <u>already formed</u> an
    BC
    opinion <u>about</u> his guilt or
    D
    innocence. <u>No error</u>
    E

17. <u>While</u> the American
    A
    Revolutionary Army
    <u>was encamped</u> at Valley Forge
    B
    <u>during</u> the bitter <u>winter months</u>
    CD
    of 1777–78. <u>No error</u>
    E

18. If anyone <u>should</u> telephone
    AB
    while I am out, tell <u>them</u> to <u>call</u>
    CD
    back after six tonight. <u>No error</u>
    E

19. If John <u>was</u> our leader, what
  A   B
<u>would he do</u> about our
  C
membership, <u>which has been</u>
  D
declining all year? <u>No error</u>
  E

20. Our neighbors told <u>us</u> that they
  A
<u>enjoyed</u> relaxing on the deck
  B
chairs, meeting <u>new</u> friends on
  C
board ship, and <u>to visit</u> different
  D
Caribbean ports. <u>No error</u>
  E

21. During a heavy <u>rainstorm</u>, the
  A   B
water <u>leaks</u> through the bricks
  C
<u>as well as</u> the roof. <u>No error</u>
  D   E

22. It was <u>him</u> <u>whom</u> I wanted to
  A   B   C
call when the police arrested
me for a crime

<u>which I did not commit</u>. <u>No error</u>
  D   E

23. The book <u>which</u> <u>was laying</u> on
  A   B
my desk has disappeared; I am
sure that someone <u>has stolen it</u>.
  C   D
<u>No error</u>
  E

24. John's <u>parents'</u> reaction to <u>his</u>
  A   B
failing the chemistry examination
<u>was expected</u> to be severe,
  C
<u>because</u> they had ordered him to
  D
prepare for it. <u>No error</u>
  E

25. After the exterminator <u>leaves</u> the
  A   B
premises, do you think we will be
<u>rid from</u> the rats and roaches
  C
<u>which</u> plague us? <u>No error</u>
  D   E

Directions: In each sentence below, some or all of the words are underlined. The portion underlined may be correct or it may contain an error in grammar, diction, style, or punctuation. The sentence is followed by five possible ways of writing the underlined portion. If you think the underlined portion is correct in the original sentence, you will choose (A) as your answer, because (A) repeats the underlined section. If you think the underlined portion is incorrect, you will select the group of words from choices (B), (C), (D), or (E) which best corrects the error you have found. Do not select a choice which changes the meaning of the original sentence.

Example: Although <u>I calculate that he will be here</u> any minute, I cannot wait much longer for him to arrive.

(A) Although I calculate that he will be here

(B) Although I reckon that he will be here

(C) Because I calculate that he will be here

(D) Although I am confident that he will be here

(E) Because I am confident that he will be here

The correct answer is (D).

26. According to zoologists, the lagomorph is <u>unlike any other rodent</u> in its dentition.

 (A) unlike any other rodent

 (B) unlike any other of the rodents

 (C) opposite to the other rodents

 (D) contrasted to the other rodents

 (E) opposite of any other rodent

27. <u>Unless they reverse present policies</u> immediately, the world may suffer permanent damage from the unregulated use of pesticides.

 (A) Unless they reverse present policies

 (B) Unless present policies are reversed

 (C) Unless present policies will be reversed

 (D) If it will not reverse present policies

 (E) If present policies will not be reversed

28. <u>Once finally he had formulated</u> the basic principles of passive resistance, Gandhi was able to teach India, and in time the world, the revolutionary power of non-violence.

 (A) Once finally he had formulated

 (B) Once he finally had formulated

 (C) When formulating, finally,

 (D) His finally having formulated

 (E) With the formulating, finally,

29. Sam Brown is one of those teachers <u>who is always ready</u> to assist new members of the faculty.

 (A) who is always ready

 (B) who always ready is

 (C) who are always ready

 (D) whom always are ready

 (E) which are always ready

30. <u>If I was he</u>, I would apologize for my insolent statement.

 (A) If I was he

 (B) If I was him

 (C) If I were him

 (D) If I were he

 (E) Had I been him

31. <u>Rodents, to some a source of disease and plague, to others</u> a source of knowledge about mammalian physiology and psychology.

 (A) Rodents, to some a source of disease and plague, to others

 (B) Although rodents are to some a source of disease and plague, to others

 (C) A source of disease and plague to some; to others, rodents

 (D) To some, rodents are a source of disease and plague; to others, they are

 (E) Some find rodents a source of disease and plague, and to others

32. In the oil shortages of the 1970's, the supply of fuel in many American cities sank to <u>such a low level that</u> service stations restricted the number of hours per day that they would sell fuel.

(A) such a low level that

(B) such a low level but

(C) such a low level so that

(D) so low a level and

(E) so low a level so that

33. Anyone interested in computer programming can find a job in contemporary industry <u>if you learn</u> the basic programming languages, such as COBOL and FORTRAN.

(A) if you learn

(B) if you will learn

(C) if he would learn

(D) by the study of

(E) by studying

34. By working overtime two nights a week, <u>his salary grew to the point</u> where he was able to buy a car.

(A) his salary grew to the point

(B) his salary grew

(C) he raised his salary to the point

(D) his salary reached the point

(E) he had his salary grow

35. <u>Being as I had studied for the examination with my friends</u>, I was not afraid.

(A) Being as I had studied for the examination with my friends

(B) Being as my friends and I had studied for the examination

(C) Since I with my friends was studying for the examination

(D) Because I had studied for the examination with my friends

(E) Being that my friends and I had studied for the examination

36. An early proponent of nuclear disarmament, <u>the Reagan administration's views on nuclear stockpiling horrified Hayden</u>.

(A) the Reagan administration's views on nuclear stockpiling horrified Hayden

(B) Hayden's horror was directed at the administration's views on nuclear stockpiling

(C) Hayden was horrified by the Reagan administration's views on nuclear stockpiling

(D) the Reagan administration's views on nuclear stockpiling were horrifying to Hayden

(E) Hayden horrified the Reagan administration's views which were on nuclear stockpiling

37. <u>More than any animal</u>, the wolverine exemplifies the unbridled ferocity of "nature red in tooth and claw."

    (A) More than any animal
    (B) More than any other animal
    (C) More than another animal
    (D) Unlike any animal
    (E) Compared to other animals

38. The reviewer knew that Barbara Cartland had written several Gothic <u>novels, she didn't remember any of their titles</u>.

    (A) novels, she didn't remember any of their titles
    (B) novels, however she didn't remember any of their titles
    (C) novels, their titles, however, she didn't remember
    (D) novels without remembering any of their titles
    (E) novels, but she remembered none of their titles

39. I think the United States will veto the resolution imposing sanctions against Israel <u>regardless of the desires of the Arab nations</u> for strong action.

    (A) regardless of the desires of the Arab nations
    (B) irregardless of the Arab nations' desires
    (C) regardless of the Arab nations desires
    (D) irregardless of the Arab nation's desires
    (E) mindful of the desires of the Arab nations

40. The Secretary of State reminded his listeners that this country <u>always has and always will honor</u> its commitments.

    (A) always has and always will honor
    (B) has always and will always honor
    (C) always has honored and always will honor
    (D) always has honored and will always
    (E) has always honored and will always

Directions: In each of the sentences below, there are four underlined words or phrases. If you think there is an error in usage, grammar, diction, or punctuation in any of the underlined parts, write the letter indicated on your answer paper. If there is no error in any of the underlined parts, mark (E) on your answer paper.

> **Example:** The <u>aircraft</u> carrier with all her <u>accompanying</u> ships are <u>going</u> to sail to the
> ‎   A   B   C
> <u>Persian Gulf</u>. <u>No error</u>
> ‎   D   E
> The correct answer is (C).

41. My mother <u>along with</u> my
    ‎   A
    brother and sister <u>insist</u> that I
    ‎   B
    continue <u>attending</u> school until
    ‎   C
    <u>graduation</u>. <u>No error</u>
    ‎   D   E

42. Because he was <u>living</u> in his
    ‎   A   B
    apartment <u>for</u> four years, his
    ‎   C
    landlord <u>agreed</u> to paint the
    ‎   D
    premises. <u>No error</u>
    ‎   E

43. The subway cars in New York
$\overline{A}$
City are as filthy as those in any
$\qquad\overline{B}\quad\overline{C}$
other metropolitan area in this
$\overline{D}$
country. No error
$\qquad\overline{E}$

44. Romeo thought that his wife

of only a few hours
$\overline{A}$
had died, however, she had taken
$\overline{B}\qquad\qquad\overline{C}$
a sleeping potion and was in a
$\qquad\qquad\qquad\overline{D}$
coma. No error
$\quad\overline{E}$

45. To write a good friendly letter is
$\quad\overline{A}\quad\overline{B}$
often more difficult than talking
$\overline{C}\qquad\qquad\overline{D}$
to a friend on the phone.

No error
$\overline{E}$

46. To protect yourself in case of
$\qquad\overline{A}$
fire, smoke detectors
$\quad\overline{B}$
should be installed in every
$\qquad\overline{C}\qquad\overline{D}$
home and hotel room in the

country. No error
$\qquad\overline{E}$

47. Every pupil in the class except
$\qquad\overline{A}\qquad\qquad\overline{B}$
her and Mary was absent from
$\qquad\overline{C}$
school at least one day this

month because of the flu.
$\qquad\overline{D}$

No error
$\overline{E}$

48. Upon entering the hospital
$\qquad\overline{A}$
emergency ward, the smell of the
$\overline{B}$
disinfectants and the sight of the
$\qquad\overline{C}$
wounded nauseated me. No error
$\qquad\overline{D}\qquad\qquad\overline{E}$

49. Susan was an excellent
$\qquad\overline{A}$
salesperson, but she was very
$\qquad\overline{B}\qquad\qquad\overline{C}$
poor at keeping records. No error
$\qquad\overline{D}\qquad\qquad\overline{E}$

50. After listening to the
$\qquad\overline{A}$
extemporaneous speeches

delivered by Mary, Helen, and
$\overline{B}$
John, the judges awarded first
$\qquad\qquad\overline{C}$
prize to the former. No error
$\qquad\qquad\overline{D}\qquad\overline{E}$

STOP
END OF TYPICAL TEST D

Answer Key—Typical Test D

1.	A	11.	C	21.	D	31.	D	41.	B
2.	B	12.	E	22.	B	32.	A	42.	B
3.	A	13.	B	23.	B	33.	E	43.	E
4.	E	14.	C	24.	E	34.	C	44.	B
5.	C	15.	B	25.	C	35.	D	45.	A
6.	A	16.	C	26.	A	36.	C	46.	A
7.	A	17.	A	27.	B	37.	B	47.	E
8.	D	18.	D	28.	B	38.	E	48.	A
9.	B	19.	B	29.	C	39.	A	49.	E
10.	E	20.	D	30.	D	40.	C	50.	D

Item Classification Chart—Typical Test D

Error	Question	See Page
Fragment	17, 31	47, 75
Run-on	38, 44	75
Subject-verb Agreement	1, 7, 13, 29, 41	76
Pronoun-Antecedent Agreement	18, 27, 33	76
Pronoun Reference		
Case	2, 22	27, 54 76
Unclear Placement of Modifier	14	58, 59
Dangling Modifier	6, 34, 36, 46, 48	77
Parallel Structure	8, 20, 21, 45	60, 77
Sequence of Tenses	16, 42	57
Mood	19, 30	58
Verb Conjugation	5, 9, 40	30
Transitive – Intransitive Verbs	23	39
Adjective Comparison	15, 37	43, 76
Adjective–Adverb Confusion	3	77
Double Negative	11	62
Diction	28, 35, 39, 50	77
Idiomatic Expression	25	65
No Error in Question	4, 10, 12, 24, 26, 32, 43, 47, 49	

How Well Did You Do on Typical Test D?

1. Find your raw score.

   a. Count the number of correct answers.

   b. Count the number of incorrect answers. (Do not count blanks as incorrect answers.)

   c. Use this formula to find your raw score:

   Raw Score = Number Correct − ¼ Number Incorrect

   Example: A student answers 41 questions correctly. He answers seven incorrectly and leaves two questions unanswered. His raw score is 41 − 1.75 (one-fourth of 7) which equals 39.25.

2. Evaluate your raw score.

Raw Score	Evaluation
45 to 50	Superior
39 to 44	Above average
33 to 38	Average
15 to 32	May need remedial work in college
Below 15	Definitely needs remedial work

How Can You Profit from This Test?

1. Look at the explanation of answers which follows this page. Notice the areas where you made your errors.

2. Chapters 3–5 of this book contain a review of the important elements of grammar, diction, style, and punctuation covered in this test. Study the sections which discuss the areas where you made your errors. If you scored low on this test, you should review all thfee chapters.

3. Go on to Typical Test E.

Answers Explained—Typical Test D

1. **A**   Error in agreement. The subject of the sentence is the singular pronoun *one*. Change *have* to *has*.

2. **B**   Error in case. Change *whomever* to the subjective case *whoever*, since *whoever* is the subject of the verb *provided*.

3. **A**   Misuse of adjective for adverb. Change *real* to *really* or *very*.

4. **E**   Choices (A), (B), (C), and (D) are all correct.

5. **C**   Incorrect past participle. Change *has brung* to *has brought*.

6. **A**   Dangling participle. The modifying phrase seems to refer to *the speeding vehicle*, which is obviously not intended. Change *chasing* to *when it chased*.

7. **A**   Error in agreement. The subject *collection*, which is singular, requires a singular verb. Change *are* to *is*.

8. **D**   Lack of parallel structure. Change *he could swim* to *to swim*, so that it will correspond to the other two infinitive phrases.

9. **B**   *Ought* is a defective verb; that is, it has no other form. Therefore, change *had ought* to *ought*.

10. **E**   Choices (A), (B), (C), and (D) are all correct.

11. **C**   *Wasn't* is incorrect for two reasons. First, it does not agree with the plural subject *candles*. Second, the expression *wasn't scarcely* is a double negative. Change *wasn't* to *were*.

12. **E**   Choices (A), (B), (C), and (D) are all correct.

13. **B**   Error in agreement. Change *is* to *are*, to agree with the plural subject *ways*.

14. **C** Squinting modifier. It is not clear whether the trip to Los Angeles or the Disneyland outing was requested by the children. Move *at the request of my children* to the end of the sentence.

15. **B** Incorrect comparative form of the adjective. Change *more lovelier* to *lovelier.*

16. **C** Error in tense. The past perfect tense is needed to show that one action (the forming of an opinion) occurred before another action (the attending of the trial). Change *already formed* to *had already formed.*

17. **A** Sentence fragment. Dropping *while* will correct this error.

18. **D** Error in agreement. The antecedent of the pronoun *them* is *anyone*, which is singular. Change *them* to *him.*

19. **B** Incorrect mood. Change *was* to the subjunctive *were* to indicate that a condition contrary to fact is being described: John is *not* the leader.

20. **D** Lack of parallel structure. Change *to visit* to *visiting*, to parallel *relaxing* and *meeting.*

21. **D** Omission of an important word. Change *as well as the roof* to *as well as through the roof.*

22. **B** Error in case. The copulative verb *was* should be followed by a predicate nominative. Change *him* to *he.*

23. **B** Misuse of transitive verb. Change *was laying* to *was lying.*

24. **E** Choices (A), (B), (C), and (D) are all correct.

25. **C** Error in idiom. The verb *to rid* should be followed by the preposition *of.*

26. **A** Choice (B) is unsatisfactory because of the awkward phrase *of the rodents.* Choices (C) and (E) change the meaning of the original sentence. The phrase *contrasted to* cannot be used as shown in choice (D).

27. **B** Choice (A) suffers from the use of the ambiguous pronoun *they.* It is not clear whom *they* is supposed to refer to. The use of the future tense in choices (C), (D), and (E) is incorrect.

28. **B** The placement of *finally* is best in choice (B). Choice (E) needs the addition of *of.*

29. **C** The antecedent of *who* is *teachers* (plural). The verb, therefore, should be the plural *are.* In choice (D), *whom* is in the wrong case. In choice (E), the word *which* is wrong, since it can not be used to refer to people.

30. **D** Choices (A) and (B) are incorrect because the verb should be in the subjunctive mood. Choices (C) and (E) are incorrect because the complement of the copulative verb *to be* should be in the nominative case.

31. **D** Choices (A), (B), and (C) are sentence fragments. Choice (E) supplies a verb, but it makes the second clause very unclear.

32. **A** In choice (B), *but* is used incorrectly. The expression *so that* in choices (C) and (E) is idiomatically incorrect. In choice (D), the word *and* is incorrectly used.

33. **E** Choices (A) and (B) suffer from the change of persons from (*anyone* to *you*). In choice (C), *would learn* is the wrong tense. The word *following* in choice (D) should not be followed by *such as.*

34. **C** Choices (A), (B), and (D) result in dangling participles. Choice (E) obscures the meaning of the sentence.

35. **D** *Being as* and *being that* in choices (A), (B), and (E) are idiomatically incorrect. Choice (C) changes the meaning of the sentence by changing the tense of the verb.

36. **C** Choices (A), (B), and (D) suffer from a dangling phrase. Choice (E) changes the meaning of the sentence.

37. **B** Choice (B) includes the necessary word *other*, which makes the comparison correct. Choice (D) changes the meaning of the sentence by its implication that the wolverine is *not* an animal.

38. **E** Choices (A), (B), and (C) are run-on sentences. Choice (D) changes the meaning of the sentence by implying that it was Barbara Cartland who could not remember the titles.

39. **A**   *Irregardless* in choices (B) and (D) is incorrect. Also, in choices (C) and (D), the case of *nations* is incorrect. The correct form of the plural possessive case of *nation* is *nations'*. Choice (E) changes the meaning of the sentence; in fact, it reverses it.

40. **C**   Improper ellipsis. The two verbs should not be cut short because they are not in the same tense.

41. **B**   Error in agreement. The subject of the verb is *mother* (singular), so the verb should be *insists* (singular).

42. **B**   Error in tense. Change *was living* to the past perfect tense *had been living* to indicate that the action had occurred before another action (the landlord's agreeing to paint).

43. **E**   Choices (A), (B), (C), and (D) are all correct.

44. **B**   Run-on sentence. The comma after *died* should be changed to a semicolon.

45. **A**   Lack of parallel structure. Change *to write* to *writing* to parallel *talking*.

46. **A**   Dangling modifier. One way of correcting this would be to change *to protect yourself* to *as a protection*.

47. **E**   Choices (A), (B), (C), and (D) are all correct.

48. **A**   Dangling modifier. Change to *When I entered the hospital emergency ward,* to make clear who is entering.

49. **E**   Choices (A), (B), (C), and (D) are all correct.

50. **D**   Misuse of word. *Former* and *latter* should be used only when discussing two items. When more than two are being discussed, use *first* and *last*.

answer sheet—typical test e

To the student:

Take the following test under examination conditions.

Have on hand a supply of #2 pencils and a good eraser.

Limit yourself to thirty minutes.

Because you will be penalized for wrong answers, do not guess wildly. However, if you can eliminate some of the choices, you can improve your score by guessing.

The answer grid below is provided for your convenience. Fill in the oval which contains the letter of your choice. You may remove this page from the book for ease in marking your answers.

1. Ⓐ Ⓑ Ⓒ Ⓓ Ⓔ   14. Ⓐ Ⓑ Ⓒ Ⓓ Ⓔ   27. Ⓐ Ⓑ Ⓒ Ⓓ Ⓔ   40. Ⓐ Ⓑ Ⓒ Ⓓ Ⓔ
2. Ⓐ Ⓑ Ⓒ Ⓓ Ⓔ   15. Ⓐ Ⓑ Ⓒ Ⓓ Ⓔ   28. Ⓐ Ⓑ Ⓒ Ⓓ Ⓔ   41. Ⓐ Ⓑ Ⓒ Ⓓ Ⓔ
3. Ⓐ Ⓑ Ⓒ Ⓓ Ⓔ   16. Ⓐ Ⓑ Ⓒ Ⓓ Ⓔ   29. Ⓐ Ⓑ Ⓒ Ⓓ Ⓔ   42. Ⓐ Ⓑ Ⓒ Ⓓ Ⓔ
4. Ⓐ Ⓑ Ⓒ Ⓓ Ⓔ   17. Ⓐ Ⓑ Ⓒ Ⓓ Ⓔ   30. Ⓐ Ⓑ Ⓒ Ⓓ Ⓔ   43. Ⓐ Ⓑ Ⓒ Ⓓ Ⓔ
5. Ⓐ Ⓑ Ⓒ Ⓓ Ⓔ   18. Ⓐ Ⓑ Ⓒ Ⓓ Ⓔ   31. Ⓐ Ⓑ Ⓒ Ⓓ Ⓔ   44. Ⓐ Ⓑ Ⓒ Ⓓ Ⓔ
6. Ⓐ Ⓑ Ⓒ Ⓓ Ⓔ   19. Ⓐ Ⓑ Ⓒ Ⓓ Ⓔ   32. Ⓐ Ⓑ Ⓒ Ⓓ Ⓔ   45. Ⓐ Ⓑ Ⓒ Ⓓ Ⓔ
7. Ⓐ Ⓑ Ⓒ Ⓓ Ⓔ   20. Ⓐ Ⓑ Ⓒ Ⓓ Ⓔ   33. Ⓐ Ⓑ Ⓒ Ⓓ Ⓔ   46. Ⓐ Ⓑ Ⓒ Ⓓ Ⓔ
8. Ⓐ Ⓑ Ⓒ Ⓓ Ⓔ   21. Ⓐ Ⓑ Ⓒ Ⓓ Ⓔ   34. Ⓐ Ⓑ Ⓒ Ⓓ Ⓔ   47. Ⓐ Ⓑ Ⓒ Ⓓ Ⓔ
9. Ⓐ Ⓑ Ⓒ Ⓓ Ⓔ   22. Ⓐ Ⓑ Ⓒ Ⓓ Ⓔ   35. Ⓐ Ⓑ Ⓒ Ⓓ Ⓔ   48. Ⓐ Ⓑ Ⓒ Ⓓ Ⓔ
10. Ⓐ Ⓑ Ⓒ Ⓓ Ⓔ   23. Ⓐ Ⓑ Ⓒ Ⓓ Ⓔ   36. Ⓐ Ⓑ Ⓒ Ⓓ Ⓔ   49. Ⓐ Ⓑ Ⓒ Ⓓ Ⓔ
11. Ⓐ Ⓑ Ⓒ Ⓓ Ⓔ   24. Ⓐ Ⓑ Ⓒ Ⓓ Ⓔ   37. Ⓐ Ⓑ Ⓒ Ⓓ Ⓔ   50. Ⓐ Ⓑ Ⓒ Ⓓ Ⓔ
12. Ⓐ Ⓑ Ⓒ Ⓓ Ⓔ   25. Ⓐ Ⓑ Ⓒ Ⓓ Ⓔ   38. Ⓐ Ⓑ Ⓒ Ⓓ Ⓔ
13. Ⓐ Ⓑ Ⓒ Ⓓ Ⓔ   26. Ⓐ Ⓑ Ⓒ Ⓓ Ⓔ   39. Ⓐ Ⓑ Ⓒ Ⓓ Ⓔ

chapter 11

typical test e

Time: 30 minutes   50 questions

Directions: In each of the sentences below, there are four underlined words or phrases. If you think there is an error in usage, grammar, diction, or punctuation in any of the underlined parts, write the letter indicated on your answer paper. If there is no error in any of the underlined parts, mark (E) on your answer paper.

Example: The aircraft carrier with all her accompanying ships are going to sail to the
                             A   B   C

Persian Gulf. No error
     D   E
The correct answer is (C).

---

1. People like you and I are often
         A   B

   overlooked when the time comes

   for promotion in the firm

   because we are so quiet. No error
           C   D   E

2. The San Francisco Opera

   along with the ballet are the basis
     A   B
   of cultural life in the Bay area
              C
   and its surrounding counties.
           D
   No error
    E

3. Swollen by the rains which
         A

   had fallen for more than thirty-
      B   C
   six hours, the river threatened

   to overflow its banks and flood
              D
   the surrounding farmlands.

   No error
    E

4. Please be quiet this afternoon, as
              A

   I am very tired and I am going to
       B   C
   lay down and take a nap.
    D
   No error
    E

5. The members played many card
   _____
   A
   games in the club room, bridge
   ____   ____
   B   C
   was the most popular. No error
   ____   _____
   D   E

6. I have, as you know, became
   _____   _____
   A   B
   accustomed to the foul weather

   which makes life so unbearable
   _____   ___
   C   D
   at this time of the year. No error
                               _____
                                  E

7. I am sorry to tell you that I
   ____   _____
   A   B
   am going to miss the meeting
   _____
   C
   due to circumstances beyond my
   _____
   D
   control. No error
            _____
               E

8. Neither the bank officials nor the
   _____
   A
   teller were able to identify the
   _____
        B
   bandit who held up the bank
              _____
                 C
   at noon today. No error
   _____   _____
      D   E

9. The SEC has announced that it

   will investigate the source of the
   _____
        A
   news leaks which led to the
            _____
              B
   sudden and unwarranted rise in
   _____   ____
     C   D
   the price of the stock. No error
                            _____
                               E

10. I believe Mike's story as much as
                        _____
                           A
    I would believe him telling me
                   ____
                    B
    that he was the King of England.
    ____   _____
     C   D
    No error
    _____
       E

11. One of my many friends who are
           ___   ____
            A   B
    not going to the football game

    tomorrow afternoon is Mary
    _____   ___
       C   D
    Elizabeth. No error
               _____
                  E

12. John was angry because of me
             _____ _____ _____
               A   B   C
    telling his mother about his
                          _____
                            D
    behavior in class. No error
                       _____
                          E

13. At his advanced age, he found
          _____   _____
             A   B
    driving to the supermarket less
                            _____
                              C
    strenuous than to walk. No error
                  _____   _____
                     D   E

14. Had I known of your interest in
    _____
         A
    philately, I would of shown you
              _____
                    B
    the stamps which I collected
                      _____
                          C
    during my many years in Europe.
             ____
               D
    No error
    _____
       E

15. In this city there is no better
                      __
                       A
    restaurants than the ones
    _____   ____
        B   C
    operated by the chef who
                        ____
                         D
    founded the chain. No error
                       _____
                          E

16. I would do exactly the same
    _____   ____
        A   B
    thing if I was in her position
            _____
              C
    of trust and responsibility.
    _____
        D
    No error
    _____
       E

17. Since Ruth is more intelligent
    _____
      A
    than any other student in the
    ____   _____
     B   C
    school, she should win at least
                           _____
                              D
    one of the prizes which will be

    awarded on Commencement

    Day. No error
        _____
           E

18. The police had arrived on the
               _____
                    A
    scene almost as soon as the
                 _____
                    B
    burglar alarm had sounded.
    _____   _____
       C   D
    No error
    _____
       E

19. Although he was still in pain, he
     $\overline{}$ $\overline{}$
        A   B
    felt some better after the
        $\overline{}$ $\overline{}$
          C   D
    operation. No error
                $\overline{}$
                    E

20. As the setting sun slowly sank
     $\overline{}$ $\overline{}$
     A   B
    behind the towering mountains
              $\overline{}$
                 C
    with their snow-covered peaks.
              $\overline{}$
                    D
    No error
    $\overline{}$
       E

21. This gourmet shop carries food
                     $\overline{}$
                        A
    of higher quality and having a
       $\overline{}$ $\overline{}$
        B   C
    lower price than the
              $\overline{}$
                 D
    supermarket. No error
                 $\overline{}$
                     E

22. Don't blame yourself for our
              $\overline{}$ $\overline{}$ $\overline{}$
        A   B   C
    failure in this venture; it is I who

    is at fault. No error
    $\overline{}$ $\overline{}$
     D   E

23. Dashing after the criminal whom
    $\overline{}$ $\overline{}$
       A   B
    he had recognized, the
       $\overline{}$
          C
    policeman ran into an elderly
               $\overline{}$
                 D
    man. No error
         $\overline{}$
            E

24. Of all the gifts which I have
    $\overline{}$ $\overline{}$
     A   B
    received, the one Mrs. O'Donnell
              $\overline{}$
                 C
    gave me is the most loveliest.
                    $\overline{}$
                       D
    No error
    $\overline{}$
       E

25. Thinking that I had done poorly
    $\overline{}$ $\overline{}$
       A   B
    on the examination, all hopes of
                       $\overline{}$
                          C
    winning the medal were
    $\overline{}$
             D
    abandoned. No error
               $\overline{}$
                  E

Directions: In each sentence below, some or all of the words are underlined. The portion underlined may be correct or it may contain an error in grammar, diction, style, or punctuation. The sentence is followed by five possible ways of writing the underlined portion. If you think the underlined portion is correct in the original sentence, you will choose (A) as your answer, because (A) repeats the underlined section. If you think the underlined portion is incorrect, you will select the group of words from choices (B), (C), (D) or (E) which best corrects the error you have found. Do not select a choice which changes the meaning of the original sentence.

Example: Although I calculate that he will be here any minute, I cannot wait much longer for him to arrive.

   (A)   Although I calculate that he will be here

   (B)   Although I reckon that he will be here

   (C)   Because I calculate that he will be here

   (D)   Although I am confident that he will be here

   (E)   Because I am confident that he will be here

   The correct answer is (D).

26. Together with Harvard, Stanford is the first choice of most knowledgeable business school candidates.

    (A)   Together with Harvard, Stanford is the first choice
    (B)   Harvard, like Stanford, are the first choices
    (C)   Stanford, together with Harvard, is the first choice
    (D)   Stanford, as well as Harvard, are the first choices
    (E)   Stanford and Harvard are the first choices

27. When one studies Latin or similar highly-inflected languages, you find word order generally less important than word endings in conveying meaning.

    (A)   When one studies Latin or similar highly-inflected languages, you find
    (B)   When you study Latin or similar highly-inflected languages, you would find
    (C)   Studying Latin or similar highly-inflected languages, you find
    (D)   When one studies Latin and similar highly-inflected languages, you find
    (E)   Studying Latin or similar highly-inflected languages, there is found

28. Although the withdrawal symptoms of a heroin addict may be relieved by injecting methadone, the heroin addiction is merely replaced by a dependence on methadone.

    (A)   by injecting
    (B)   through injecting
    (C)   in injecting
    (D)   by injections of
    (E)   beside injections of

29. While campaigning for President, Anderson nearly exhausted his funds and must raise money so that he could pay for last-minute television commercials.

    (A)   nearly exhausted his funds and must raise money so that he could pay
    (B)   would exhaust his funds to raise money so that he could pay
    (C)   exhausted his funds and had to raise money so that he can pay
    (D)   exhausted his funds and had to raise money so that he could pay
    (E)   exhausted his funds and must raise money so that he can pay

30. Athletic coaches stress not only eating nutritious meals but also to get adequate sleep.

    (A)   not only eating nutritious meals but also to get
    (B)   to not only eat nutritious meals but also getting
    (C)   not only to eat nutritious meals but also getting
    (D)   not only the eating of nutritious meals but also getting
    (E)   not only eating nutritious meals but also getting

31. Oakland, California is where the American novelist Jack London spent his early manhood; it was a busy waterfront town.

    (A)   is where the American novelist Jack London spent his early manhood; it was a busy waterfront town
    (B)   was the busy waterfront town where the American novelist Jack London spent his early manhood
    (C)   is the place where the American novelist Jack London spent his early manhood in a busy waterfront town

(D)   is the site of the busy waterfront which was where the American novelist Jack London was situated in early manhood

(E)   is where the American novelist Jack London spent his early manhood in a busy waterfront town

32.   The goal of the remedial program was <u>that it enables</u> the students to master the basic skills they need to succeed in regular coursework.

(A)   that it enables

(B)   by enabling

(C)   to enable

(D)   where students are enabled

(E)   where it enables

33.   Her coach <u>along with her parents and friends are confident she</u> will win the tournament.

(A)   along with her parents and friends are confident she

(B)   along with her parents and friends are confident that she

(C)   along with her parents and friends have been confident she

(D)   together with her parents and friends are confident she

(E)   along with her parents and friends is confident she

34.   The referee <u>would of stopped the fight if the battered boxer would of risen</u> to his feet.

(A)   would of stopped the fight if the battered boxer would of risen

(B)   would have stopped the fight if the battered boxer would have risen

(C)   would have stopped the fight if the battered boxer had risen

(D)   would of stopped the fight if the battered boxer would of rose

(E)   would have stopped the fight if the battered boxer had rose

35.   When the waitress told me that I could have my choice of vanilla, chocolate, or pistachio ice cream, I selected <u>the former even though I prefer the latter.</u>

(A)   the former even though I prefer the latter

(B)   the first even though I prefer the latter

(C)   the former even though I prefer the last

(D)   the former even though it is the latter that I prefer

(E)   the first even though I prefer the last

36.   In visiting the Tower of London, <u>Mrs. Pomeroy's hat was blown off her head into the river.</u>

(A)   In visiting the Tower of London, Mrs. Pomeroy's hat was blown off her head into the river.

(B)   Mrs. Pomeroy visited the Tower of London, her hat blew off her head into the river.

(C)   Mrs. Pomeroy, who was visiting the Tower of London when her hat blew off her head, saw it fall into the river.

(D)   When Mrs. Pomeroy visited the Tower of London, her hat was blown off her head and fell into the river.

(E)   Mrs. Pomeroy visited the Tower of London; suddenly her hat was blown off her head which fell into the river.

37. To understand the depth of feeling against conscription existing in our country today, we must comprehend the effects of Vietnam on an entire generation of young Americans.

    (A) we must comprehend
    (B) it necessitates a comprehension of
    (C) a comprehension is needed of
    (D) there is necessitated a comprehension of
    (E) we necessitate comprehension of

38. Instead of treating patients with proper professional ethics, Dr. Molesworth is accused of issuing unnecessary prescriptions, abusing drugs, and he overcharges.

    (A) issuing unnecessary prescriptions, abusing drugs, and he overcharges
    (B) the issuance of unnecessary prescriptions, the abuse of drugs, and the overcharge of them
    (C) the issuance of unnecessary prescriptions, drug abuse, and he overcharges
    (D) issuing unnecessary prescriptions, abusing drugs, and overcharging
    (E) issuing unnecessary prescriptions, drug abuse, and overcharging

39. Because it gets very chilly in this part of the country at night, we ought to find a motel before the sun sets.

    (A) we ought to find a motel before the sun sets
    (B) we had ought to find a motel before the sun sets
    (C) we ought to find a motel before the sun sits
    (D) we should find a motel before the sun sits
    (E) we must find a motel before the sun sets

40. Mary objected to you taking sides in the dispute between Frank and I.

    (A) to you taking sides in the dispute between Frank and I
    (B) to your taking sides in the dispute between Frank and me
    (C) to your taking sides in the dispute between Frank and I
    (D) to you taking sides in the dispute among Frank and I
    (E) to your taking sides in the dispute among Frank and me

---

Directions: In each of the sentences below, there are four underlined words or phrases. If you think there is an error in usage, grammar, diction, or punctuation in any of the underlined parts, write the letter indicated on your answer paper. If there is no error in any of the underlined parts, mark (E) on your answer paper.

Example: The aircraft carrier with all her accompanying ships are going to sail to the
            ‾‾‾‾‾‾   ‾‾‾‾‾‾‾‾‾‾‾‾   ‾‾‾‾‾‾
              A   B   C
Persian Gulf. No error
‾‾‾‾‾‾‾‾‾‾‾ ‾‾‾‾‾‾‾‾
      D   E
The correct answer is (C).

41. The senators <u>are going to</u>
A
consider the <u>affect</u> that the
B
proposed tax reduction <u>will have</u>
C
on our <u>nation's</u> economy.
D
<u>No error</u>
E

42. The <u>reason</u> for the poor sales of
A
<u>American-made</u> automobiles is
B
<u>because</u> the Japanese <u>imports</u>
C   D
are more economical to operate.

<u>No error</u>
E

43. When I heard the news <u>about the</u>
A
cyclone, I was <u>real</u> sorry for the
B
<u>unfortunate</u> victims who <u>had lost</u>
C   D
their homes. <u>No error</u>
E

44. <u>I wish</u> that you would give this
A
book to <u>whoever</u> will enjoy
B
<u>reading</u> a good <u>mystery</u> novel.
C   D
<u>No error</u>
E

45. I feel very <u>badly</u> about the
A
inconvenience I <u>have caused</u> by
B
my <u>inability</u> to deliver your order
C
at the <u>promised</u> time. <u>No error</u>
D   E

46. Because I did not have <u>much</u>
A   B
time after football practice, I

<u>was only able</u> to read three of the
C
essays <u>assigned</u> as homework.
D
<u>No error</u>
E

47. Frank <u>has invested</u> wisely, and
A
today he is <u>richer</u> than <u>any</u>
B   C   D
member of his community.

<u>No error</u>
E

48. If John <u>had realized</u> the
A   B
consequences of his actions, he

<u>would have behaved</u> <u>differently</u>.
C   D
<u>No error</u>
E

49. Speaking <u>against</u> the proposed
A
change in the provisions for early

retirement in the Social Security

Act <u>was</u> the <u>president</u> of the
B   C
Association of Retired Persons

and <u>several</u> members of
D
Congress. <u>No error</u>
E

50. <u>By the time</u> he was <u>apprehended</u>
A   B
by the police, <u>he already decided</u>
C
to turn <u>himself</u> in. <u>No error</u>
D   E

STOP
END OF TYPICAL TEST E

Answer Key—Typical Test E

1. B	11. E	21. C	31. B	41. B
2. A	12. C	22. D	32. C	42. C
3. E	13. D	23. E	33. E	43. B
4. D	14. B	24. D	34. C	44. E
5. C	15. A	25. A	35. E	45. A
6. B	16. C	26. E	36. D	46. C
7. D	17. E	27. C	37. A	47. D
8. B	18. A	28. D	38. D	48. E
9. E	19. C	29. D	39. A	49. B
10. B	20. A	30. E	40. B	50. C

Item Classification Chart—Typical Test E

Error	Question	See Page
Fragment	26	47, 75
Run-on	5	75
Subject-verb Agreement	2, 8, 15, 22, 26, 33, 49	76
Pronoun-Antecedent Agreement	27	76
Pronoun Reference		
Case	1, 10, 12, 40	27, 54 76
Unclear Placement of Modifier	46	58, 59
Dangling Modifier	25, 36	59, 77
Parallel Structure	13, 21, 30, 38	60, 77
Sequence of Tenses	18, 29, 50	57
Mood	16	58
Verb Conjugation	6, 34, 39	30
Transitive – Intransitive Verbs	4	39
Adjective Comparison	24, 47	43, 76
Adjective–Adverb Confusion	43, 45	77
Double Negative		
Diction	7, 14, 19, 23, 31, 32, 35, 41, 42	77
Idiomatic Expression		
No Error in Question	3, 9, 11, 17, 23, 37, 44, 48	

How Well Did You Do on Typical Test E?

1. Find your raw score.

   a. Count the number of correct answers.

   b. Count the number of incorrect answers. (Do not count blanks as incorrect answers.)

   c. Use this formula to find your raw score:

   Raw Score = Number Correct − ¼ Number Incorrect

   Example: A student answers 41 questions correctly. He answers seven incorrectly and leaves two questions unanswered. His raw score is 41 − 1.75 (one-fourth of 7) which equals 39.25.

2. Evaluate your raw score.

Raw Score	Evaluation
45 to 50	Superior
39 to 44	Above average
33 to 38	Average
15 to 32	May need remedial work in college
Below 15	Definitely needs remedial work

How Can You Profit from This Test?

1. Look at the explanation of answers which follows this page. Notice the areas where you made your errors.

2. Chapters 3–5 of this book contain a review of the important elements of grammar, diction, style, and punctuation covered in this test. Study the sections which discuss the areas where you made your errors. If you scored low on this test, you should review all three chapters.

Answers Explained—Typical Test E

1. **B**   Error in case. Change *I* to *me*, because the pronoun is the object of the preposition *like*.

2. **A**   Error in agreement caused by using the wrong connective. If we use the phrase *along with*, the sentence will require the verb *is* rather than *are*, since a singular subject requires a singular verb. However, the verb *are* may not be changed, since it is not underlined. If we change *along with* to *and*, however, we will have a plural subject, and the plural verb *are* will be correct.

3. **E**   Choices (A), (B), (C), and (D) are all correct.

4. **D**   Misuse of transitive verb. Change the transitive verb *lay* to the intransitive verb *lie*.

5. **C**   Run-on sentence. The simplest way to correct it is to change the comma to a semicolon.

6. **B**   Error in tense. The present perfect tense of *become* is *have become*.

7. **D**   Error in diction. *Due to* should not be used as a substitute for *because of*.

8. **B**   Error in agreement. In a *neither . . . nor* expression, the verb agrees with the noun or pronoun immediately preceding it. Change *were able* to *was able* to fit the singular subject *teller*.

9. **E**   Choices (A), (B), (C), and (D) are all correct.

10. **B**   Error in case. A noun or pronoun immediately preceding a gerund should be in the possessive case. Change *him* to *his*.

11. **E**   Choices (A), (B), (C), and (D) are all correct.

12. **C**   Error in case. A noun or pronoun immediately preceding a gerund should be in the possessive case. Change *me* to *my*.

13. **D**   Lack of parallel structure. Change *to walk* to *walking*.

14. **B**   Error in diction. Change *would of* to *would have*.

15. **A**   Error in agreement between subject and verb. The subject is the plural word *restaurants*; therefore, the verb should be the plural *are*.

16. **C**   Incorrect mood. The subjunctive mood is necessary when a condition contrary to fact is being described. Since I am not in her position, change *was* to *were*.

17. **E**   Choices (A), (B), (C), and (D) are all correct.

18. **A**   Error in tense. Change *had arrived* to *arrived*, to indicate that the burglar alarm went off before the police arrived.

19. **C**   Error in diction. Change the adjective *some* to the adverb *somewhat*.

20. **A**   This group of words is a sentence fragment. The deletion of *as* will create a good sentence.

21. **C**   Lack of parallel structure. Change *having* to *at*. The sentence now has two prepositional phrases modifying *food*.

22. **D**   Error in agreement. The antecedent of the pronoun *who* is *I*. Therefore, in this sentence, *who* is a first person singular pronoun and so requires a first person singular verb. Change *is* to *am*.

23. **E**   Choices (A), (B), (C), and (D) are all correct.

24. **D**   Incorrect form of the adjective. The superlative form of the adjective *lovely* is either *loveliest* or *most lovely*.

25. **A**   Dangling participle. Change *thinking* to *because I thought*.

26. **E**   Choices (B) and (D) have an error in agreement. The subject in (B) is the singular *Harvard*; therefore, the verb should be *is*. Similarly, in (D), the subject is the singular *Stanford*. The subordination of one school to the other in choices (A) and (C), while grammatically correct, does not convey the intended meaning as clearly as choice (E).

27. **C**   In choices (A) and (D), we find an unnecessary shift in the person of the pronouns from *one* to *you*. The tense of the verb *would find* in choice (B) is incorrect. Choice (E) is awkward and vague, since it does not specify who is to do the finding.

28. **D**   Choices (A), (B), and (C) convey the idea that one injection of methadone is sufficient to create an addiction. Choice (E) does not make sense.

29. **D**   Choices (A), (B), (C), and (E) suffer from errors in the sequence of tenses.

30. **E**   A lack of parallel structure is found in the other four choices.

31. **B**   Choice (B) is the clearest, most graceful, and most concise way of expressing the ideas being described.

32. **C**   Choice (A) provides us with the result of the program rather than the goal. Choice (B) results in a sentence fragment. Choices (D) and (E) use the *was where* construction, which is unclear and should be avoided.

33. **E**   Choices (A), (B), (C), and (D) suffer from an error in agreement between the subject and the verb. Remember that the prepositional phrase *along with her parents and*

friends is not part of the subject. The subject is the singular word *coach*; it should be followed by the singular verb *is*.

34. **C** The use of *of* instead of *have* in choices (A) and (D) is incorrect. The *if* clause requires the subjunctive mood *had risen* instead of *would have risen* in choice (B). Choices (D) and (E) are incorrect, because the past participle of *rise* is *risen*.

35. **E** *Former* and *latter* should be used only when two items are under consideration. When three or more items are discussed, as in this sentence, use *first* and *last*.

36. **D** Choice (A) is unacceptable because of the dangling modifier. Choice (B) is a run-on sentence. Choice (C) changes the meaning of the sentence. Choice (E) suffers from a misplaced modifier. Did her head fall into the river? So choice (E) would imply.

37. **A** Choices (B), (C), (D), and (E) are too involved. Choice (A) is a clear and simple statement.

38. **D** The other choices suffer from a lack of parallel structure.

39. **A** *Had ought* in choice (B) is incorrect; the verb *ought* is not inflected. Choices (C) and (D) confuse the verbs *sit* and *set*. Choice (E) changes the meaning of the sentence.

40. **B** Choice (A) contains two errors in the case of the pronouns. The pronoun preceding a gerund should be in the possessive case, so that *you* should be changed to *your*; the pronoun which is the object of a preposition should be in the objective case, so that *I* should be changed to *me*. Choice (B) corrects both errors. Choice (E) also corrects the two errors; however, it misuses *among*, which should be used only when three or more people or things are involved.

41. **B** Error in diction. *Effect* is the correct word in this sentence.

42. **C** Error in diction. Always use the construction *The reason . . . is that* instead of *The reason . . . is because*.

43. **B** Misuse of adjective when an adverb is called for. Change *real* to *really* or *very*.

44. **E** Choices (A), (B), (C), and (D) are all correct.

45. **A** Misuse of adverb when an adjective is called for. Copulative verbs like *feel* should be followed by a predicate adjective instead of by an adverb. Change *badly* to *bad*.

46. **C** Misplaced word. *Only* should come as close to the word it limits as possible. In this sentence, it should come immediately before *three*.

47. **D** Faulty comparison. Change *any* to *any other*, since Frank himself is a member of his community.

48. **E** Choices (A), (B), (C), and (D) are all correct.

49. **B** Lack of agreement between subject and verb. The compound subject (*president* and *members*) calls for a plural verb. Change *was* to *were*.

50. **C** Faulty sequence of tenses. Change *decided* to *had decided*.

index